Wonderful Mu[illegible]

Christmas

MW00768883

Project Manager: Carol Cuellar
Cover Design: Odalis Soto

© 1997 WARNER BROS. PUBLICATIONS
All Rights Reserved

Any duplication, adaptation or arrangement of the compositions
contained in this collection requires the written consent of the Publisher.
No part of this book may be photocopied or reproduced in any way without permission.
Unauthorized uses are an infringement of the U.S. Copyright Act and are punishable by law.

Contents

ROCKIN' AROUND THE CHRISTMAS TREE

By JOHNNY MARKS

© 1958 (Renewed 1986) ST. NICHOLAS MUSIC, INC.
All Rights Reserved Used by Permission

F G#dim F G#dim F Em Am E+
You will get a sen - ti - men - tal feel - ing when you hear voic - es sing - ing,
Am7 D7 G7 C
"Let's be jol - ly, Deck the halls with boughs of hol - ly" ROCK-IN' A-ROUND THE
sfz f mp
G7 G9 G7
CHRIST-MAS TREE. Have a hap - py hol - i - day.
Ev - 'ry - one danc - ing
G9 G7 G9 1. G7 G7-9 Dm7 G7 C 2. G7 G7-9
mer - ri - ly in the new old fash - ioned way. new old
Dm7 G7 C
fash - ioned way.
f dim. poco a poco p sfz
Ped

LET IT SNOW! LET IT SNOW! LET IT SNOW!

Lyric by
SAMMY CAHN

Music by
JULE STYNE

© 1945 CAHN MUSIC COMPANY
Copyright Renewed and Assigned to CAHN MUSIC COMPANY and PRODUCERS MUSIC PUB. CO., INC.
All Rights on behalf of CAHN MUSIC COMPANY Administered by WB MUSIC CORP.
All Rights on behalf of PRODUCERS MUSIC PUB. CO., INC. Administered by CHAPPELL & CO.
All Rights Reserved

Gm D+ D7 Gm A♭dim C7 F
lights are turned 'way down low. LET IT SNOW! LET IT SNOW! LET IT SNOW! When we
f
mf
C C♯dim Dm7 G7 C
fin - al - ly kiss good - night, How I'll hate go - ing out in the storm! But if
C B+ Gm A7 D7 G7 C F C7
you'll real - ly hold me tight All the way home I'll be warm. The
mf
F C7 F A♭dim C7 D7
fi - re is slow - ly dy - ing And, my dear, we're still good - bye - ing, But as
G D+ D7 Gm A♭dim C7 1. F 2. F
long as you love me so LET IT SNOW! LET IT SNOW'! LET IT SNOW! Oh the SNOW!
f
mf
sfz

JINGLE BELLS

JAMES PIERPONT

© 1973 (Assigned) WARNER BROS. PUBLICATIONS INC.
All Rights Reserved including Public Performance for Profit

Chorus:
D7
G
D7
G
sleigh - ing song to - night! Jin - gle bells, jin - gle bells, jin - gle all the
D7
G
A7
way, Oh, what fun it is to ride in a one - horse o - pen
D7
G
sleigh! Jin - gle bells, jin - gle bells, jin - gle all the way,
D7
G
D7
G
Oh, what fun it is to ride in a one - horse o - pen sleigh!

SLEIGH RIDE

Words by
MITCHELL PARISH

Music by
LEROY ANDERSON

Moderately bright
f
mf
G
Am7
D7
Bb
Just hear those sleigh bells jin - gle - ing, ring - ting - tin - gle - ing, too,
Come on, it's love - ly weath - er for a Sleigh Ride to-geth - er with you,
Out - side the snow is fall - ing and friends are call - ing "Yoo hoo,"

© 1948, 1950 (Renewed 1976, 1978) EMI MILLS MUSIC, INC.
Print Rights on behalf of EMI MILLS MUSIC, INC. Administered by WARNER BROS. PUBLICATIONS U.S. INC.
All Rights Reserved

Am7
D7
G
Come on, it's love - ly weath - er for a Sleigh Ride to - geth - er with you.
C♯m7
F♯7
B
Gid - dy - yap, gid - dy - yap, gid - dy - yap, let's go,
Let's look at the show,
We're rid - ing in a won - der - land of snow.
Bm
Gid - dy - yap, gid - dy - yap, gid - dy - yap, it's grand,
Bm7
E7
A
Just hold - ing your hand.
We're glid - ing a - long with a song of a win - ter - y fair - y - land, Our cheeks are nice and ros - y, and

Am7 D7 G Am7 D7 G
com - fy co - zy are we, We're snug - gled up to - geth - er like two
Am7 D7 G B♭ D7 G
birds of a feath - er would be. Let's take that road be - fore us and
Am7 D7 G Am7 D7 G
sing a cho - rus or two. Come on, it's love - ly weath - er for a
Am7 D7 1. G C G D7
Sleigh Ride to - geth - er with you. Just hear those
2. G
you.
dim.
p f

ANGELS FROM THE REALMS OF GLORY

JAMES MONTGOMERY

By HENRY SMART

Moderately
C
F
C
Am
G7
C
mf
1. An - gels from the realms of glo - ry, Wing your flight o'er all the earth,

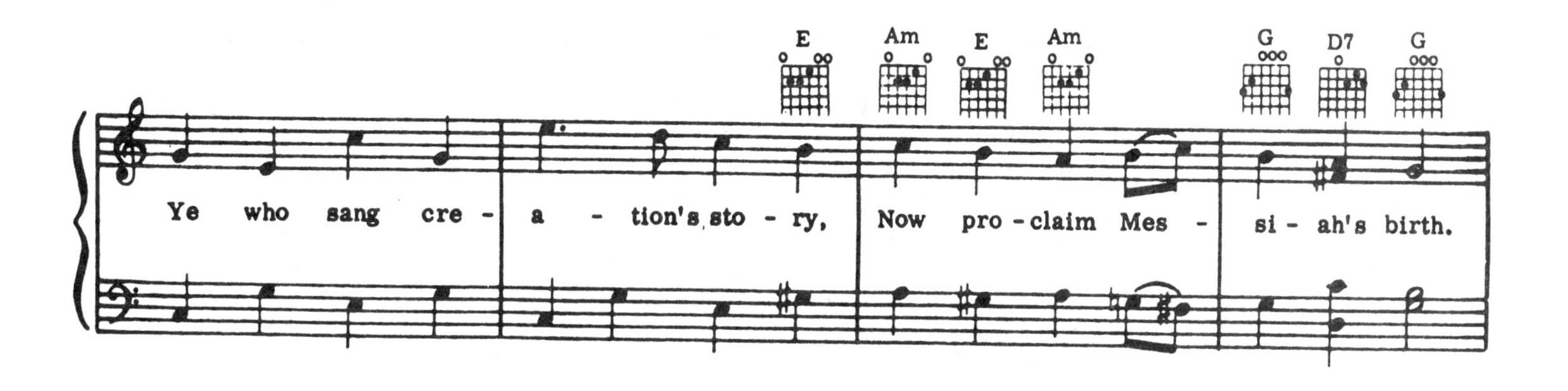
E
Am
E
Am
G
D7
G
Ye who sang cre - a - tion's sto - ry, Now pro - claim Mes - si - ah's birth.

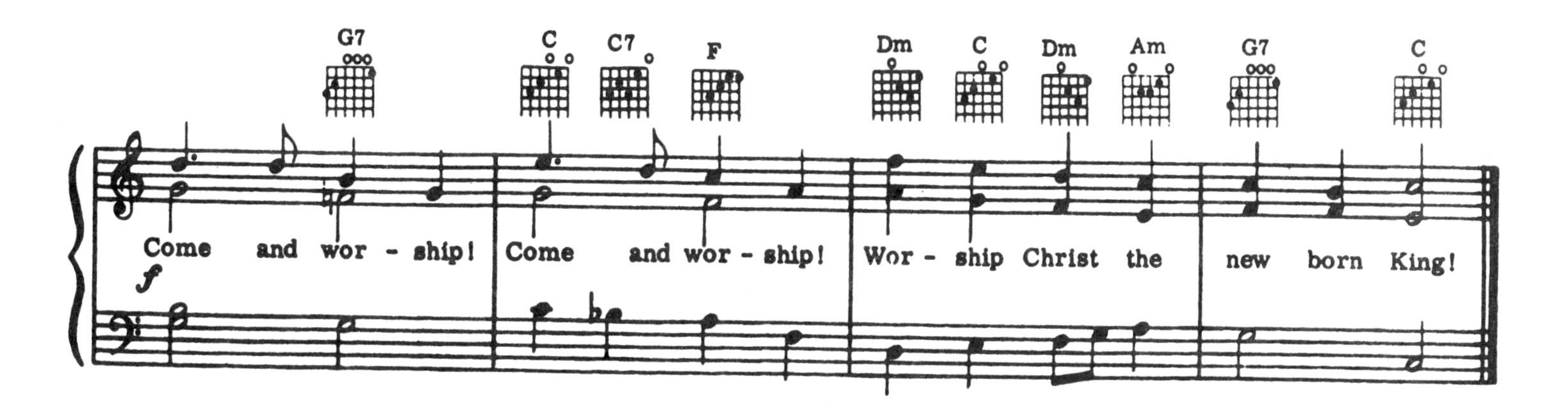
G7
C
C7
F
Dm
C
Dm
Am
G7
C
f
Come and wor - ship! Come and wor - ship! Wor - ship Christ the new born King!

2. Shepherds in the fields abiding,
Watching o'er your flocks by night,
God with man is now residing
Yonder shines the infant Light.
Come and worship! etc.

3. Sages, leave your contemplations
Brighter visions beam afar,
Seek the great Desire of nations
Ye have seen His natal star.
Come and worship! etc.

© 1965 (Renewed & Assigned) WARNER BROS. PUBLICATIONS INC.
All Rights Reserved including Public Performance for Profit

ALL I WANT FOR CHRISTMAS IS MY TWO FRONT TEETH

Words and Music by
DON GARDNER

© 1946, 1947 WARNER BROS. INC.
Copyrights Renewed
All Rights Reserved

C D7 G7 C C7
Gee, if I could on-ly have my two front teeth, then I could wish you, "Mer-ry Christ-mas" It
F Dm7 F#o7 Ebo7 C G7 C E7
seems so long since I could say, "Sis-ter Su-sie sit-ting on a this-tle!"
Am E7 Am E7 Am Am7 D7 G7 C
Gosh oh gee, how hap-py I'd be, if I could on-ly whis-tle (thhh.) All I want for Christ-mas is MY
fz
mp
D7 G7 C C7
TWO FRONT TEETH, my two front teeth, see my two front teeth. Gee, if I could on-ly have my
F F#o7 C G7 C G7 G6 G7 C G7 Cmaj9 C6
two front teeth, then I could wish you "Mer-ry Christ-mas!" I could wish you "Mer-ry Christ-mas!"
cresc.

AMAZING GRACE

Traditional

Moderate

G D♯dim Em C

A - maz - ing grace! How sweet the
Through man - y dan - gers, toils and

G D7 G

sound That saved a wretch like me! I
snares, I have al - read - y come. 'Tis

C G Em G

once was lost, but now am found; Was blind, but
grace hath brought me safe thus far, And grace will

mf

© 1972 (Assigned) WB MUSIC CORP. (ASCAP)
All Rights Administered by WARNER BROS. PUBLICATIONS U.S. INC.
All Rights Reserved including Public Performance for Profit

A7
D7
G
Gmaj7
C
G
D♯dim
now I see. 'Twas grace that taught my
lead me home. When we've been there ten
Em
C
G
D7
G
heart to fear And grace my fears re - lieved.
thou - sand years, Bright shin - ning as the sun,
C
How pre - cious did that grace ap -
We've no less days to sing God's
G
Em
G
A7
D7
C
G
D. C.
pear The hour I first be - lieved!
praise Than when we first be - gan.
Fine

ANGELS FROM HEAVEN

Translated by
BERNARD GASSO

Traditional Hungarian

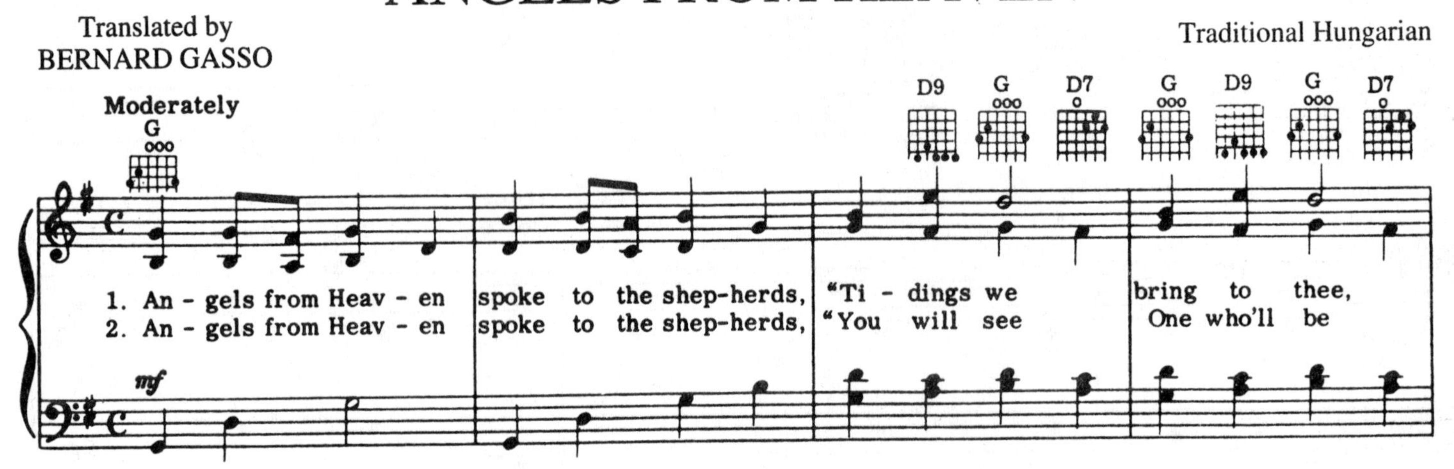
Moderately
G
D9
G
D7
G
D9
G
D7
1. An - gels from Heav - en spoke to the shep-herds, "Ti - dings we bring to thee,
2. An - gels from Heav - en spoke to the shep-herds, "You will see One who'll be
mf

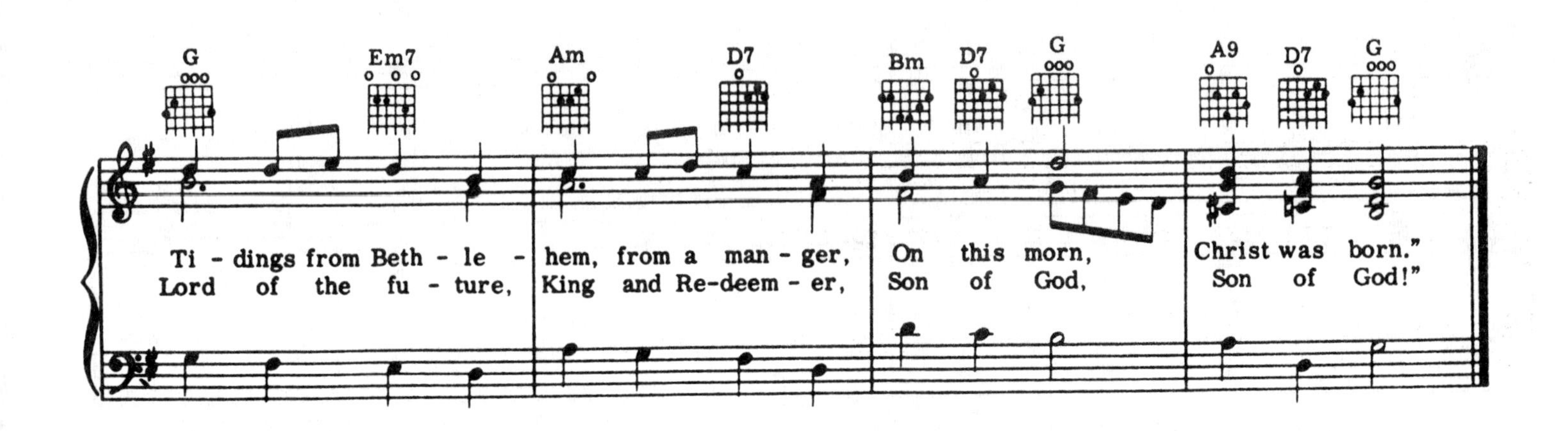
G
Em7
Am
D7
Bm
D7
G
A9
D7
G
Ti - dings from Beth - le - hem, from a man - ger, On this morn, Christ was born."
Lord of the fu - ture, King and Re-deem - er, Son of God, Son of God!"

© 1970 (Assigned) WB MUSIC CORP. (ASCAP)
All Rights Administered by WARNER BROS. PUBLICATIONS U.S. INC.
All Rights Reserved including Public Performance for Profit

AULD LANG SYNE

© 1965 (Renewed & Assigned) WARNER BROS. PUBLICATIONS INC.
All Rights Reserved including Public Performance for Profit

AWAY IN A MANGER

Words and Music by
J.E. SPILLMAN
and MARTIN LUTHER

© 1977 (Assigned) WARNER BROS. PUBLICATIONS INC.
All Rights Reserved including Public Performance for Profit

D
Em
A7
D
cat - tle are low - ing, the poor ba - by wakes, But
way in a man - ger, no crib for His bed, The
mf
G
D
A7
D
D9
lit - tle Lord Je - sus, no cry - ing He makes. I
lit - tle Lord Je - sus lay down His sweet head. The
G
D7
G
C
G
love Thee, Lord Je - sus, look down from the sky And
stars in the heav - ens looked down where He lay, The
D
G
G7
C
G
D7
G
stay by my cra - dle to watch lul - la - by.
lit - tle Lord Je - sus a - sleep in the hay.

THE BELLS OF CHRISTMAS
(Hear the Bells)

Words and Music by
MARY STUART

© 1967, 1971 (Assigned) WB MUSIC CORP. (ASCAP)
All Rights Administered by WARNER BROS. PUBLICATIONS U.S. INC.
All Rights Reserved including Public Performance for Profit

Am7
D7
G
Em
Am7
Love was born to - day,
Peace was born to - day,
brought us love this day,
And
Love was
Peace was
brought us
D7
G
Em
G
1.2.
Em
3. D.C. al Coda
Em
born to - day.
born to - day.
peace this day.
Coda
Am7
D7
G
Em
Love was born to - day,
Peace was born to - day,
Am7
D7
G
Em
Love and peace to - day,
Am7
D7
G
Love and peace this day.
rit.

THE BIRTHDAY OF A KING

By WILLIAM HOWARD NEIDLINGER

© 1978 (Assigned) WARNER BROS. PUBLICATIONS INC.
All Rights Reserved including Public Performance for Profit

G
D
Chorus
Am7
D7
place where Je - sus lay.
per - fect Ho - ly day.
Al - le - lu - ia, O how the
G
Em
A7
D7
an - gels sang! Al - le - lu - ia, how it rang and the
B7
Em
D7
G
sky was bright with a ho - ly light, twas the
D7
1. G
D
2. G
birth - day of a King. 2. 'Twas the King.

BORN IS HE, THIS HOLY CHILD

Translated by
BERNARD GASSO

French

2. See Him lying peacefully
On His tiny bed of hay;
See Him lying in stable bare,
O what gracious a Lord is there!
(Refrain)

3. Jesus! Thou all-powerful Lord,
Now as Baby art Thou adored;
Jesus! Thou all-powerful King,
All our hearts to Thee we bring.
(Refrain)

© 1970 (Assigned) WB MUSIC CORP. (ASCAP)
All Rights Administered by WARNER BROS. PUBLICATIONS U.S. INC.
All Rights Reserved including Public Performance for Profit

BRIGHT AND JOYFUL IS THE MORN

Words by
JAMES MONTGOMERY

Welsh Hymn

© 1972 (Assigned) WB MUSIC CORP. (ASCAP)
All Rights Administered by WARNER BROS. PUBLICATIONS U.S. INC.
All Rights Reserved including Public Performance for Profit

BRING A TORCH, JEANNETTE, ISABELLA

© 1981 (Assigned) WB MUSIC CORP. (ASCAP)
All Rights Administered by WARNER BROS. PUBLICATIONS U.S. INC.
All Rights Reserved including Public Performance for Profit

THE CHIPMUNK SONG
(Christmas, Don't Be Late)

By ROSS BAGDASARIAN, SR.

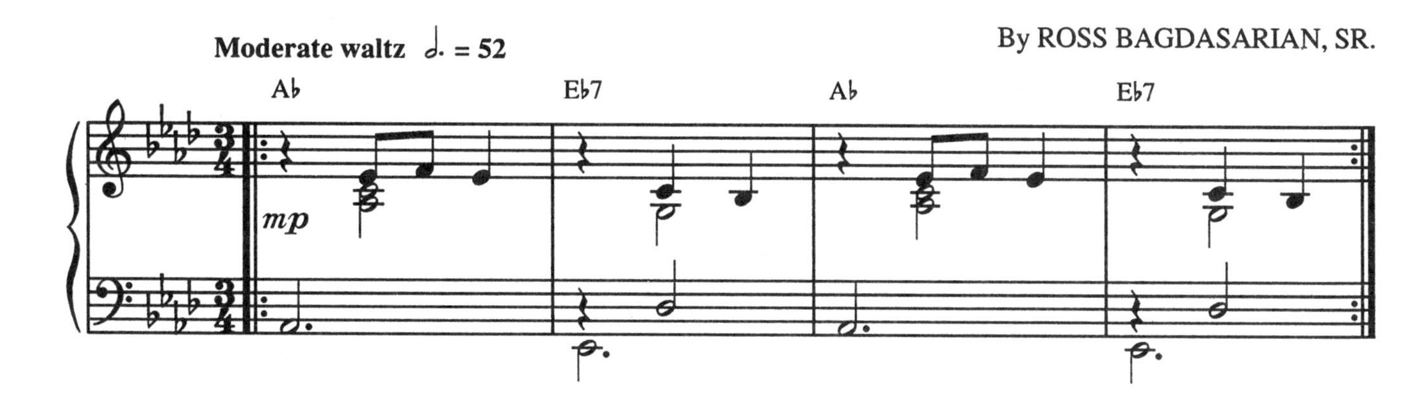
Moderate waltz ♩. = 52
Ab
Eb7
Ab
Eb7
mp

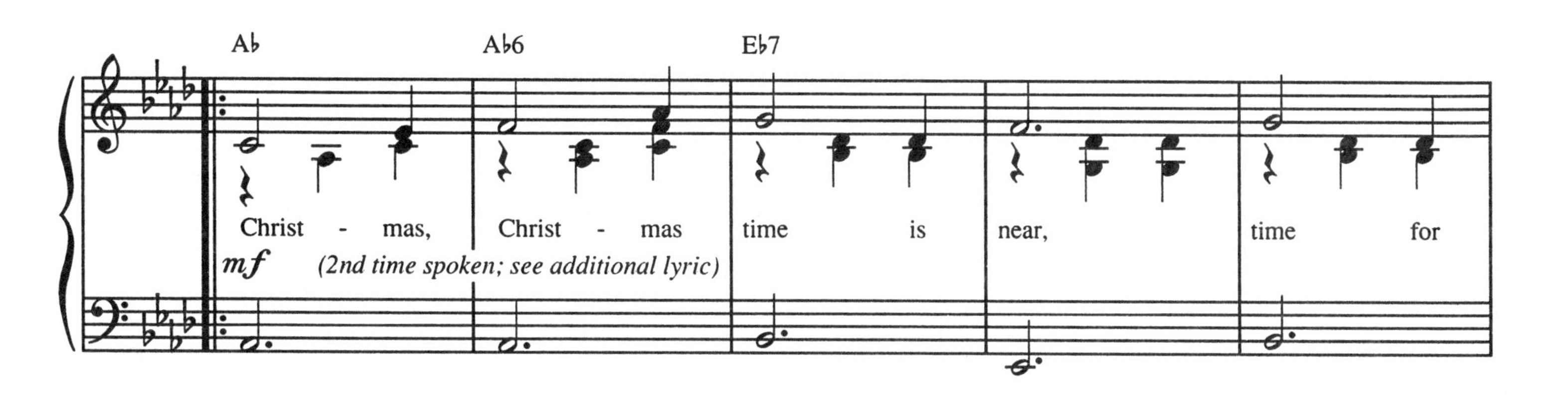
Ab
Ab6
Eb7
Christ - mas, Christ - mas time is near, time for
mf (2nd time spoken; see additional lyric)

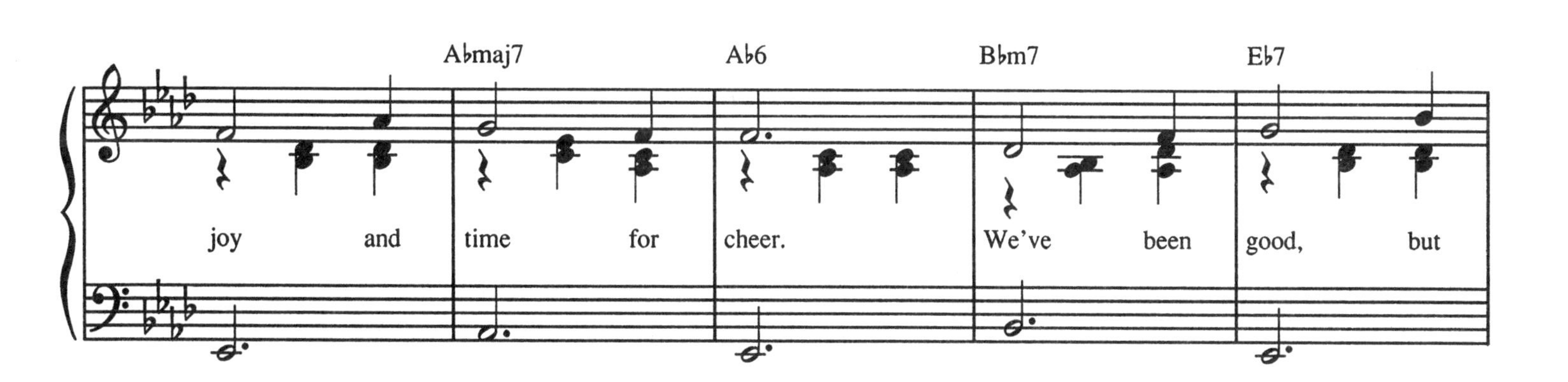
Abmaj7
Ab6
Bbm7
Eb7
joy and time for cheer. We've been good, but

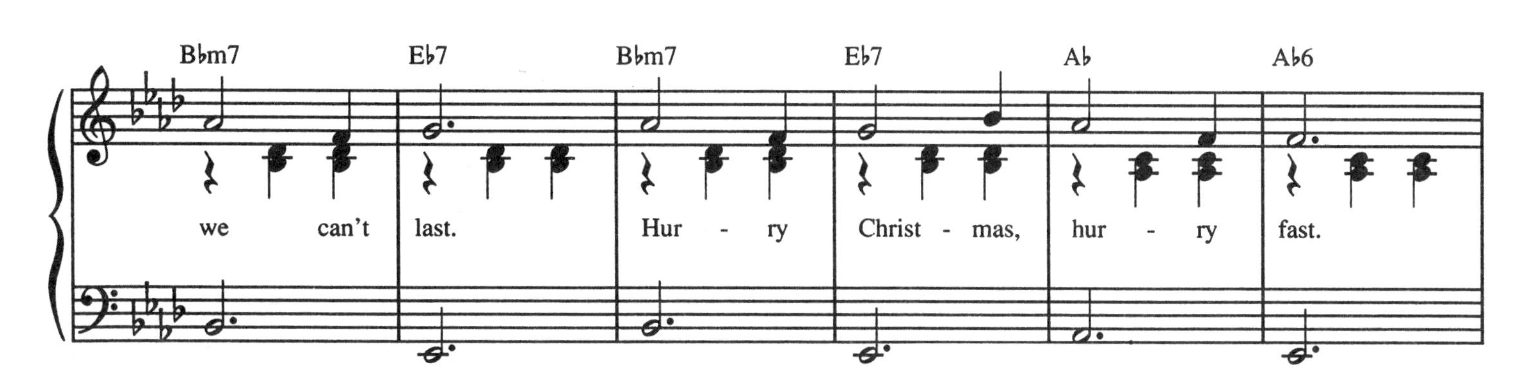
Bbm7
Eb7
Bbm7
Eb7
Ab
Ab6
we can't last. Hur - ry Christ - mas, hur - ry fast.

Copyright © 1958 (Renewed 1986) MONARCH MUSIC (BMI)
This Arrangement Copyright © 1993 MONARCH MUSIC (BMI) Used by Permission
International Copyright Secured Made in U.S.A. All Rights Reserved

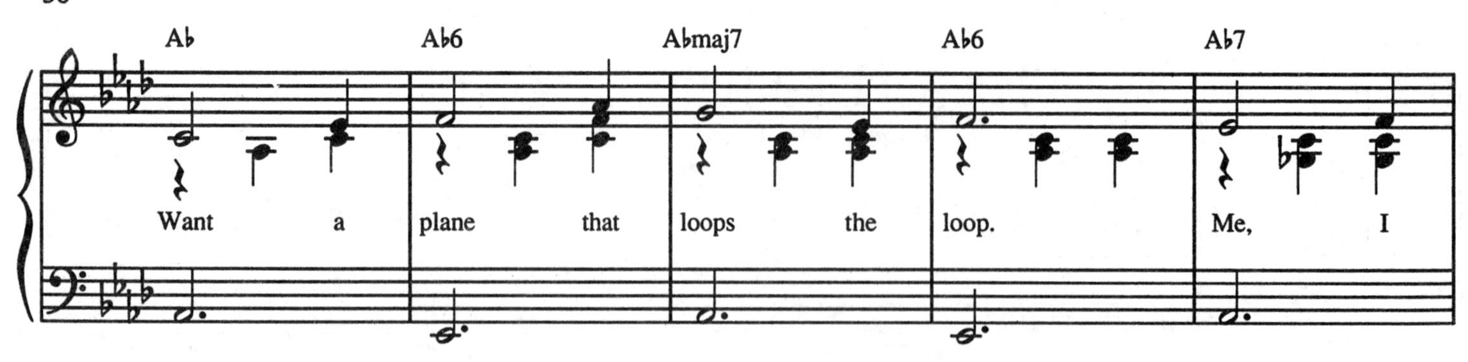
Ab
Ab6
Abmaj7
Ab6
Ab7
Want a plane that loops the loop. Me, I

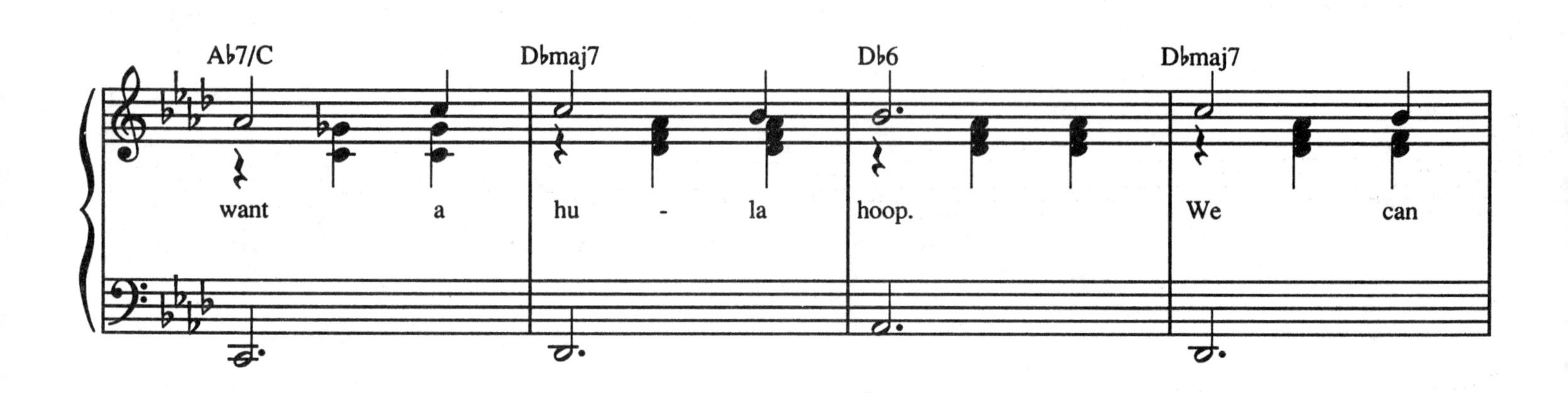
Ab7/C
Dbmaj7
Db6
Dbmaj7
want a hu - la hoop. We can

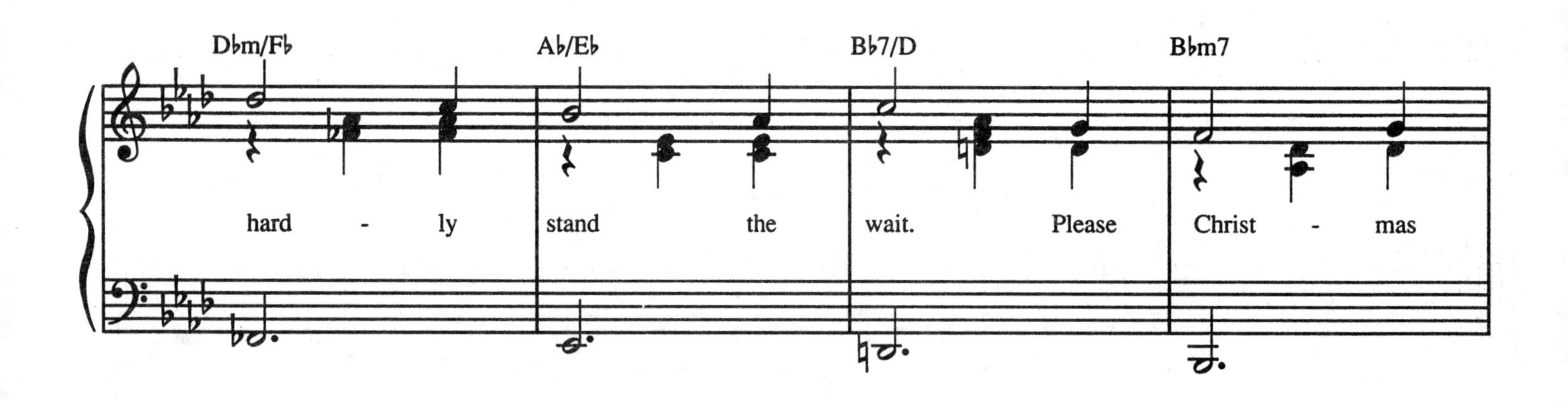
Dbm/Fb
Ab/Eb
Bb7/D
Bbm7
hard - ly stand the wait. Please Christ - mas

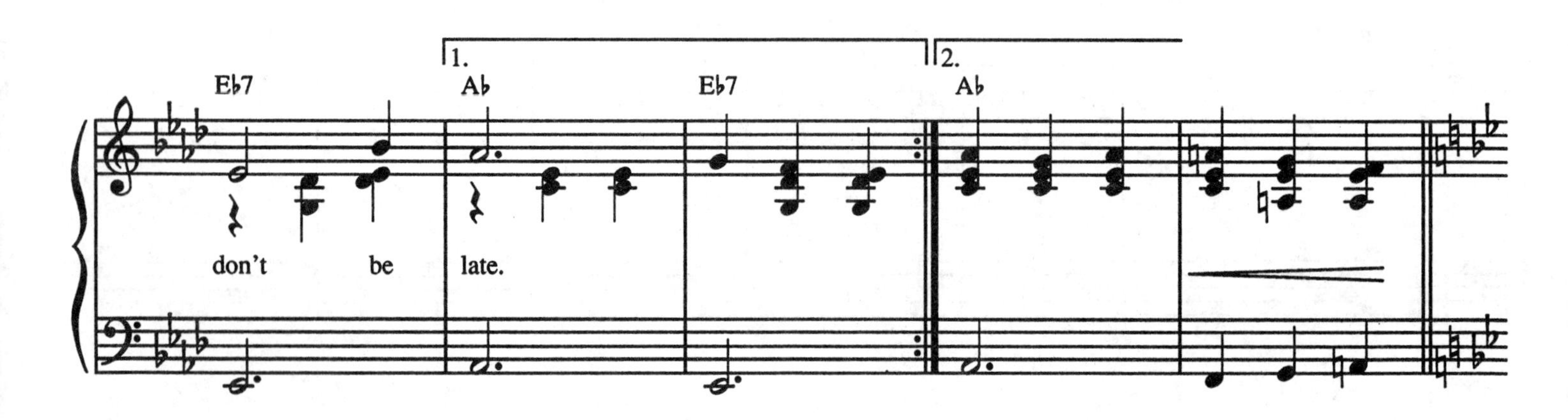
1.
2.
Eb7
Ab
Eb7
Ab
don't be late.

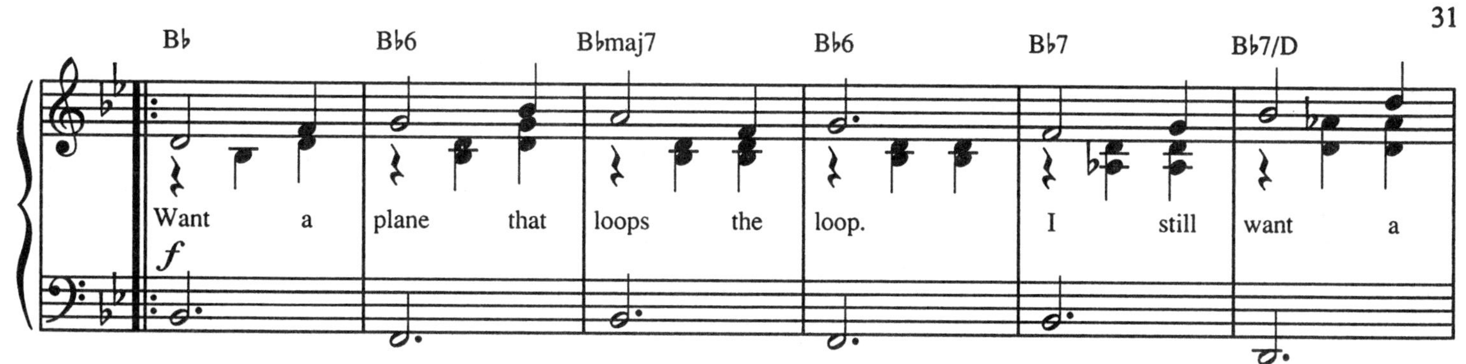

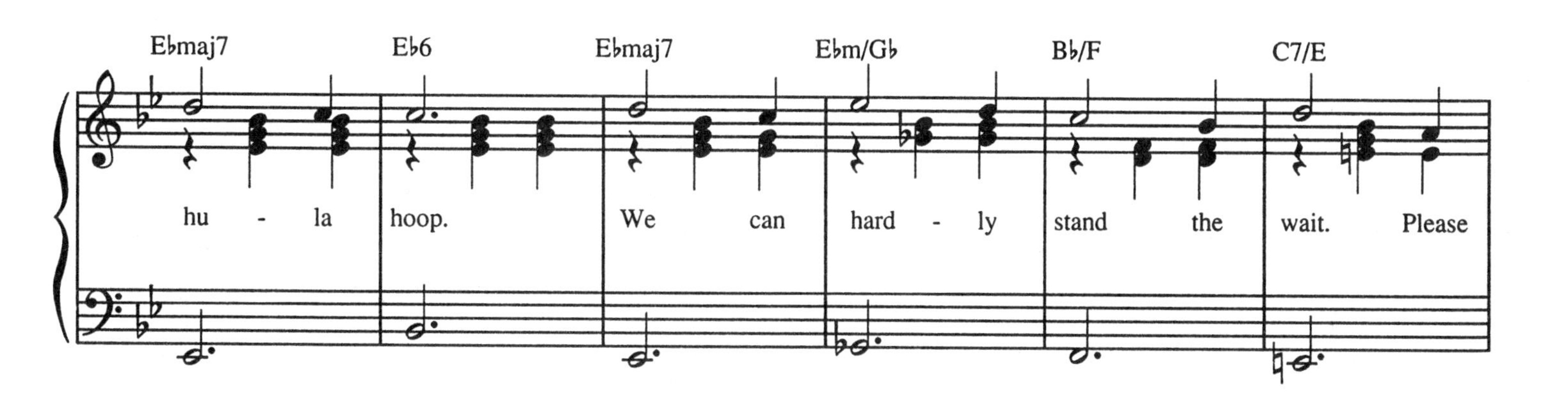

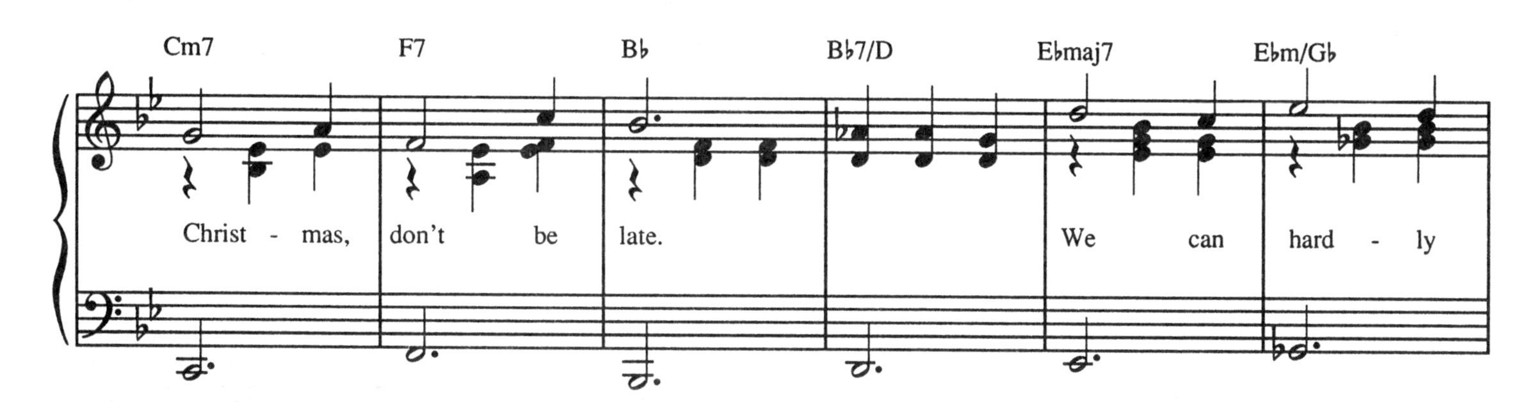

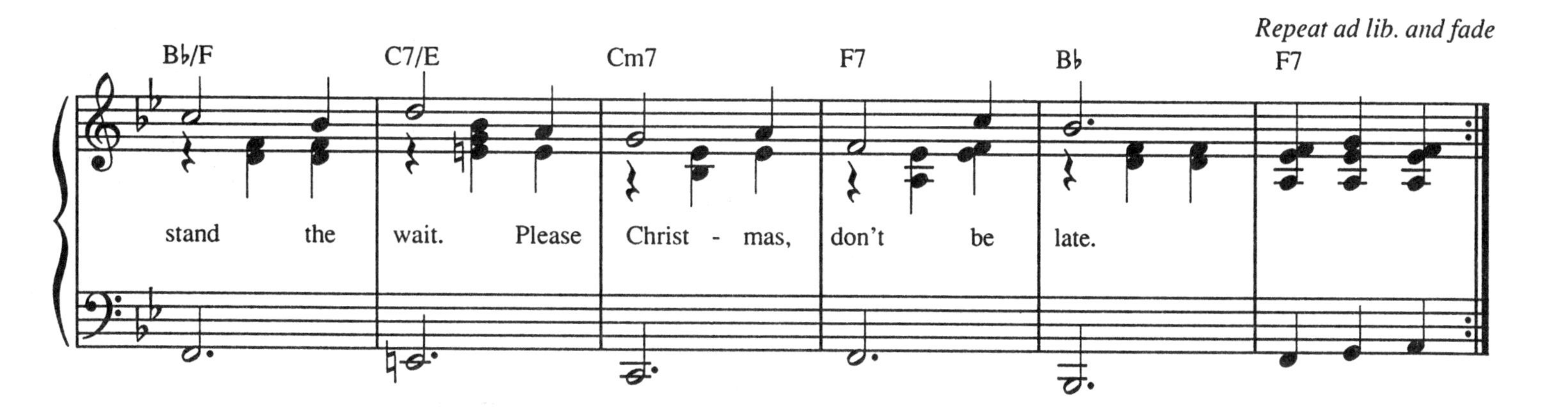

Additional lyric spoken:
Alvin: *Dave, I've been asking for that hula hoop for years.*
I would like to ask for something new,
Like roller skates, or a new stereo.
But I've just got to get that hula hoop first.
Please Dave?
I feel I've been very patient.
Dave: *Alvin, just finish the song.*
We'll talk about it later.

CHRISTMAS IN NEW ENGLAND

Words by
AUSTIN ROBERTS

Music by
JAMES PATRICK DUNNE

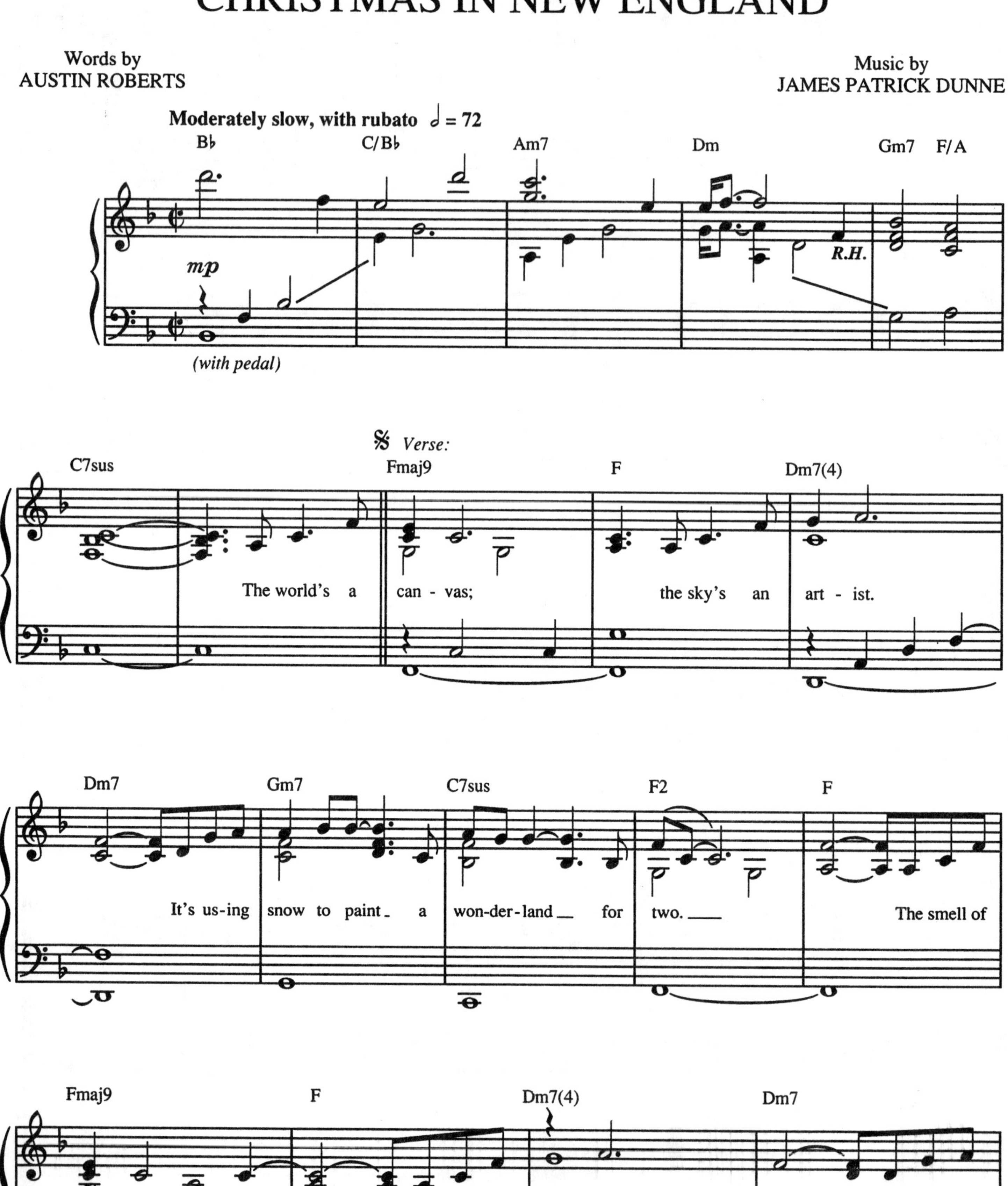

Copyright © 1987 by UNICHAPPELL MUSIC (BMI), CHRISWALD (ASCAP) and HOPI (ASCAP)
International Copyright Secured Made in U.S.A. All Rights Reserved

Gm7
C7sus
F
F7(no 3rd)
time of year will find me here with you. 'Cause there's a
B♭
A7sus
A
Dm9
G7sus
G7
mag - ic in New Eng - land that will bring us back a - gain, no
Gm7(4)
C9sus
F
Gm7(4)
F/A
mat - ter where we are or where we've been.
cresc.
Chorus:
B♭
C/B♭
Am7
Dm7
Gm7
mf
Christ-mas in New Eng - land; there's no - where else on
C7sus
C7
F(2)
Gm7
F/A
B♭(2)
C/B♭
earth I'd rath-er be. Christ-mas in New

Am7
A7
Dm7
Gm7
C7sus
Eng - land with you, a dream that keeps com-ing true for

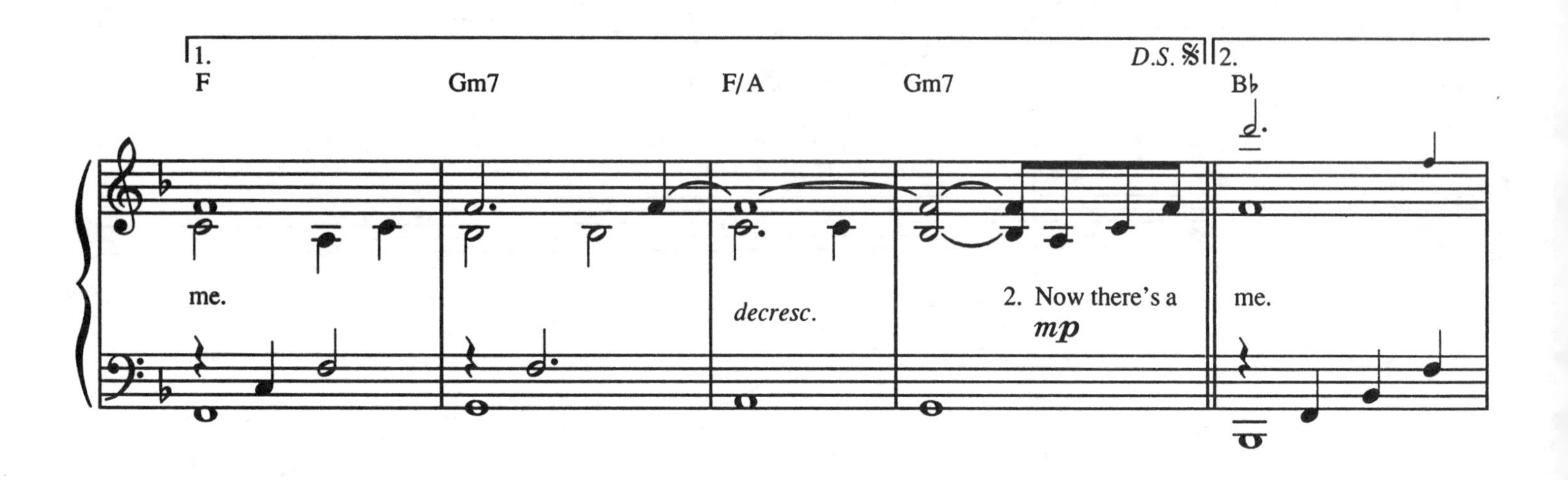
1.
D.S. 𝄋
2.
F
Gm7
F/A
Gm7
B♭
me.
decresc.
2. Now there's a
mp
me.

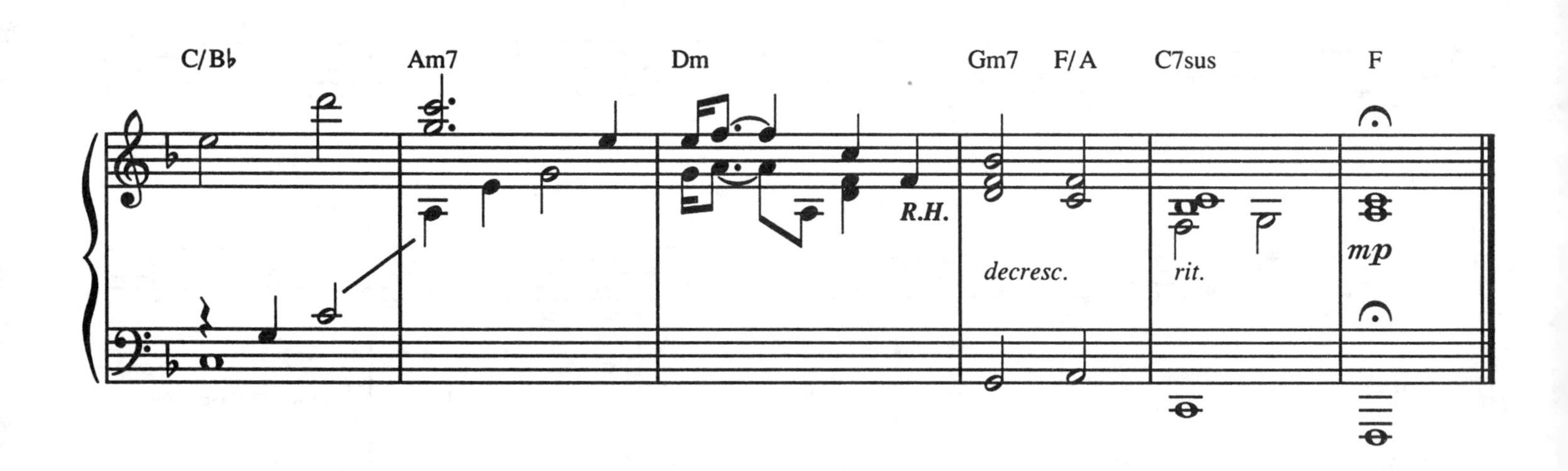
C/B♭
Am7
Dm
Gm7
F/A
C7sus
F
R.H.
decresc.
rit.
mp

Verse 2:
Now there's a candle in every window.
I love to see the light reflecting in your eyes.
Walking down Main Street feels so familiar;
I hold your hand and know why true love never dies.
And coming home to spend the holidays
Is one thing time can't change.
The feeling here will always be the same.
(To Chorus:)

COME, ALL YE SHEPHERDS

Czech Carol

Gaily

F Bb F Bb F C7 F

1. Come, all ye shepherds such wonders enthrall.

F Bb F Bb F C7 F

Come where the young Child is laid in a stall.

F Am Dm C7 F Am Dm C7

This day to us a Savior is given. Whom God on high hath sent down from heaven.

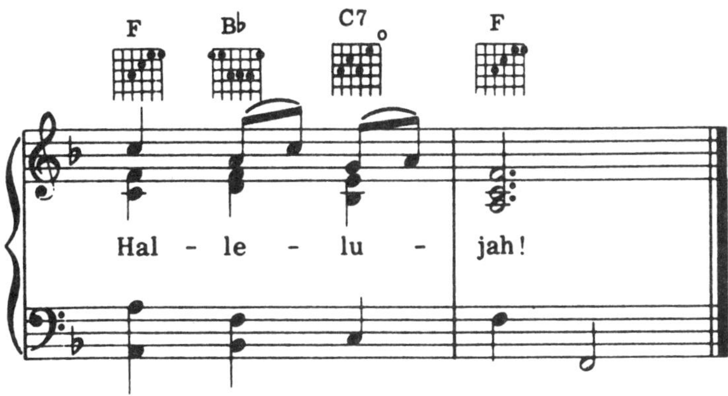

2. Come hear what wonderful tidings are fraught.
   In Bethlehem see what joy they have brought.
   Good will from heaven to man is given,
   Peace never ending to earth descending,
   Glory to God!

3. Haste then to Bethlehem, there to behold
   Jesus the Babe of whom angels have told.
   There to His glory tell we the story,
   Glad voices raising Him over praising,
   Hallelujah!

© 1969 (Assigned) WB MUSIC CORP. (ASCAP)
All Rights Administered by WARNER BROS. PUBLICATIONS U.S. INC.
All Rights Reserved including Public Performance for Profit

CHRISTMAS TIME OF THE YEAR

Words by
JOE COCUZZO

Music by
JOE COCUZZO and TORRIE ZITO

© 1984, 1986 JOSEPH G. COCUZZO & TORRIE ZITO
All Rights Reserved

1.
Fm7
B♭7
Gm7
3fr.
Cm7
3fr.
child - ren list - en, for Dan - cer and Blitz-en, and the
p
Cm7/F
8fr.
F13
10fr.
B♭maj7
B♭7/D
3fr.
bells on San - ta's sleigh. The
E♭
Cm7
3fr.
F7-5
B♭7
eve of Christ - mas day, all the
2.
Fm7
B♭7
Gm7
3fr.
Cm7
3fr.
snow - flakes fly, they catch your eye, like
p cresc.

Cm7/F
8fr.
F13
10fr.
Fm7/Bb
Bb13-9
6fr.
dia - monds_ in the sky._ And the
mf
Eb6/9/Bb
5fr.
Bbm7/Eb
Abmaj7
4fr.
Fm/Ab
F/A
church bells ring. And the choirs_ sing. For
dance; let's sing. Let the Church bells ring. For
Last time to Coda
G/B
G7-9
Cm7
3fr.
F13
10fr.
F7
love is_ king once more. Oh, that
love and_ peace we pray. May your
Eb/Bb
D/Bb
Eb6/9/Bb
5fr.
Cm7
3fr.
Gb13
3fr.
spe - cial_ time of year is here a -

F13
10fr.
F7
F13-5
F7
Fm7/Bb
Bb7-9
gain for you and yours. So to
Eb6/9
5fr.
Ab13-5
Ab7
4fr.
Gm7
3fr.
G7
G7+5
all of you, dear friends, may this
mf
Cmaj7
Dm7/G
Cmaj7
C/E
Christ - mas be more than just a tree. Though you
mp
Fm7
Bb7
Gm7
3fr.
Cm7
3fr.
may de - ny, rein - deer in the sky, it's the
p cresc.

Cm7/F
8fr.
F13
10fr.
Fm7/B♭
B♭13-9
6fr.
D.S. al Coda
chil - dren who make them fly.
So let's
mf
Coda
E♭6/9/B♭
5fr.
Fm/A♭
4fr.
E♭/G
3fr.
chil - dren's chil - dren's chil - dren
A♭m6
A♭m6/C♭
E♭/B♭
Fm/B♭
have this gift on Christ - mas
B♭m7/E♭
B♭m7-5/E♭
A♭maj7
4fr.
day. May your chil - dren's

Fm6/Ab
Eb/G
Abm6
Abm6/Cb
chil - dren's
chil - dren
have
this
Eb/Bb
Fm/Bb
Eb6
Db6/9
gift
on
Christ - mas
day.
p
Cbmaj7
Fbmaj7-5
Eb6/9
L.H.

I SAW THREE SHIPS

Traditional English
XV Century Legend

Allegro
mf
G
D
G
D
D7
G
1. I saw three ships come sail - ing in, On Christ - mas Day, on
2. And what was in those ships all three, On Christ - mas Day, on
3. The Vir - gin Mary and Christ were there, On Christ - mas Day, on
4. Then let us all re - joice a - main, On Christ - mas Day, on
mf
D
Em
D
G
D
D7
G
C
D7
G
D
G
Christ-mas Day; I saw three ships come sail - ing in, On Christ-mas Day in the morn-ing.
Christ-mas Day; And what was in those ships all three, On Christ-mas Day in the morn-ing.
Christ-mas Day; The Vir - gin Mary and Christ were there, On Christ-mas Day in the morn-ing.
Christ-mas Day; Then let us all re - joice a - main, On Christ-mas Day in the morn-ing.

© 1958 WARNER BROS. INC. (Renewed)
All Rights Reserved

GATHER AROUND THE CHRISTMAS TREE

By
JOHN HOPKINS

Moderately

G D7 G D D7 G D7 G D D7 G
mf
Gath-er a-round the Christ-mas tree! Gath-er a-round the Christ-mas tree!
cresc.
G B7 Em Am D7 G D7 G D7 Em7 A7 D G
1. Ev-er green have its branch-es been, It is king of all the wood-land scene; For
2. Once the pride of the moun-tain side, Now cut down to grace our Christ-mas-tide: For
3. Ev-'ry bough has a bur-den now, They are gifts of love for us, we trow: For
cresc.

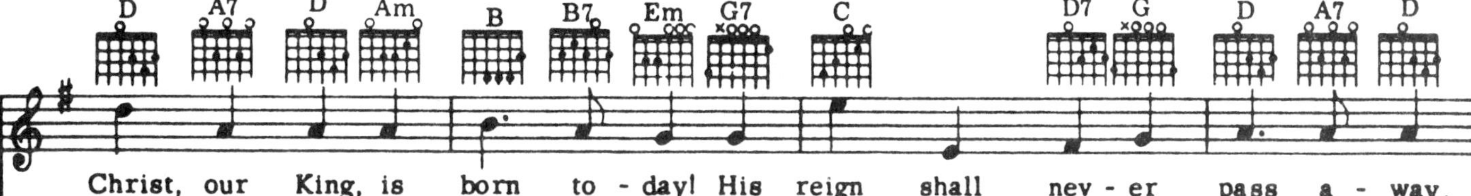
D A7 D Am B B7 Em G7 C D7 G D A7 D
Christ, our King, is born to-day! His reign shall nev-er pass a-way.
Christ from heav'n to earth came down, To gain, through death, a nob-ler crown.
Christ is born, His love to show, And give good gifts to men be-low.

CHORUS

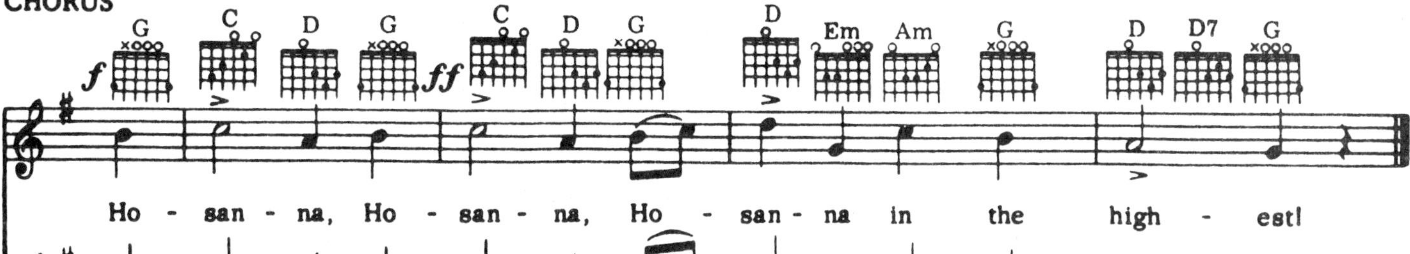
G C D G C D G D Em Am G D D7 G
f ff
Ho-san-na, Ho-san-na, Ho-san-na in the high-est!

© 1958 WARNER BROS. INC. (Renewed)
All Rights Reserved

THE COVENTRY CAROL

(Lullay, Thou Little Tiny Child)

The Coventry Carol - 2 - 1

© 1978 (Assigned) WARNER BROS. PUBLICATIONS INC.
All Rights Reserved including Public Performance for Profit

Gm
F
Bb
(D Bass)
lay. Lul - lay, thou
day. This poor young -
day. His men of
say. For thy part -
F
(C Bass)
Bb
Cm6
Cm
(Eb Bass)
D7
lit - tle ti - ny child,
ling for whom we sing,
night, in his own sight,
ing nor say, nor sing,
Gm
(Bb Bass)
D7
(A Bass)
Eb
(G Bass)
Cm
D7
G
by, by, lul - lay, lul - lay.
by, by, lul - lay, lul - lay.
all chil - dren young to slay.
by, by, lul - lay, lul - lay.

THE CHRISTMAS WALTZ

Words by
SAMMY CAHN

Music by
JULE STYNE

Copyright © 1954 SANDS MUSIC CORP.
Copyright Renewed and Assigned to CAHN MUSIC COMPANY & JULE STYNE
All rights on behalf of CAHN MUSIC COMPANY Administered by WB MUSIC CORP.
Jule Styne's interest controlled by PRODUCERS MUSIC PUB. CO. INC. and Administered by CHAPPELL & CO.
All Rights Reserved

Gm7
C7-9
Fmaj7
Dm7
G9
G7-5
filled his sleigh with things, Things for you and for
C7
C7+5
F
D7sus4
D7
Gm7
me. It's that time of year, When the world falls in
C7
F
D7-9
love, Ev - 'ry song you hear seems to
Gm
C7-9
F
say: "Mer - ry Christ - mas, May your

Gm7
C7
Am7-5
D7
D+
D7
New Year dreams come true." And this
G9
C9
C7
F
song of mine, in three - quar - ter time,
D7
G7
Cm7
C7
Wish - es you and yours the same thing
F
Dm
Gm7
C9
F
too.
poco rall.

DANCE OF THE SUGAR-PLUM FAIRY
(From "The Nutcracker Suite")

Music by
PETER ILYICH TCHAIKOVSKY

© 1969 (Assigned) WB MUSIC CORP. (ASCAP)
All Rights Administered by WARNER BROS. PUBLICATIONS U.S. INC.
All Rights Reserved including Public Performance for Profit

DECK THE HALLS

Traditional

Allegro
C7
Ddim
C
F
1. Deck the hall with boughs of hol - ly,
2. See the blaz - ing Yule be - fore us,
3. Fast a - way the old year pass - es,
mf
Gm
Fa la la la la, la la la la,
'Tis the sea - son
Strike the harp and
Hail the new, ye
to be jol - ly,
join the cho - rus,
lads and lass - es,
Fa la la la la, la

© 1974 (Assigned) WARNER BROS. PUBLICATIONS INC.
All Rights Reserved including Public Performance for Profit

F C7 F C C7 F C
la la la
Don we now our gay ap - par - rel,
Fol - low me in mer - ry meas - ure,
Sing we joy - ous all to - geth - er,
F Am Dm7 G G7 C F C7
Fa la la la la la la la,
Troll the an - cient
While I tell of
Heed - less of the
Dm C F B♭ F Gm F C7 F
Yule - tide car - ol,
Yule - tide treas - ure,
Wind and weath - er,
Fa la la la la, la la la la.

EVERYONE'S A CHILD AT CHRISTMAS

Words and Music by
JOHNNY MARKS

Moderato
Piano
l.h.
mf
Refrain (Lightly and gaily)
C
C7+5
F
Dm7
EV - 'RY-ONE'S A CHILD AT CHRIST - MAS And
mp - mf
G7
C
looks for pres-ents un-der the Christ-mas tree.
C
C7+5
F
Dm7
EV - 'RY-ONE'S A CHILD AT CHRIST - MAS And

© 1955 (Renewed 1983) ST. NICHOLAS MUSIC, INC.
All Rights Reserved

G7 C F C G7 C F♯dim
loves the hap - py hol - i - day jol - li - ty. You must
G7 C G7 Gm6 A7 D7
al - ways be - lieve, that on each Christ-mas Eve, Old San - ta
Am7 D7 G7 Gdim Dm7 G7 C
Claus will be com - ing be-cause you're good, Did ev -'ry-thing you should. EV -'RY-ONE'S A
C7+5 F Dm7 G7
CHILD AT CHRIST - MAS, For Christ-mas is for
(Opt.)
1. C G7 C6 G F Em G7
2. C G7 C
chil-dren like you and me. me.

THE FIRST NOEL

Traditional English Carol

© 1965 (Renewed & Assigned) WARNER BROS. PUBLICATIONS INC.
All Rights Reserved including Public Performance for Profit

FROM EAST TO WEST

JOHN ELLERTON

Traditional German

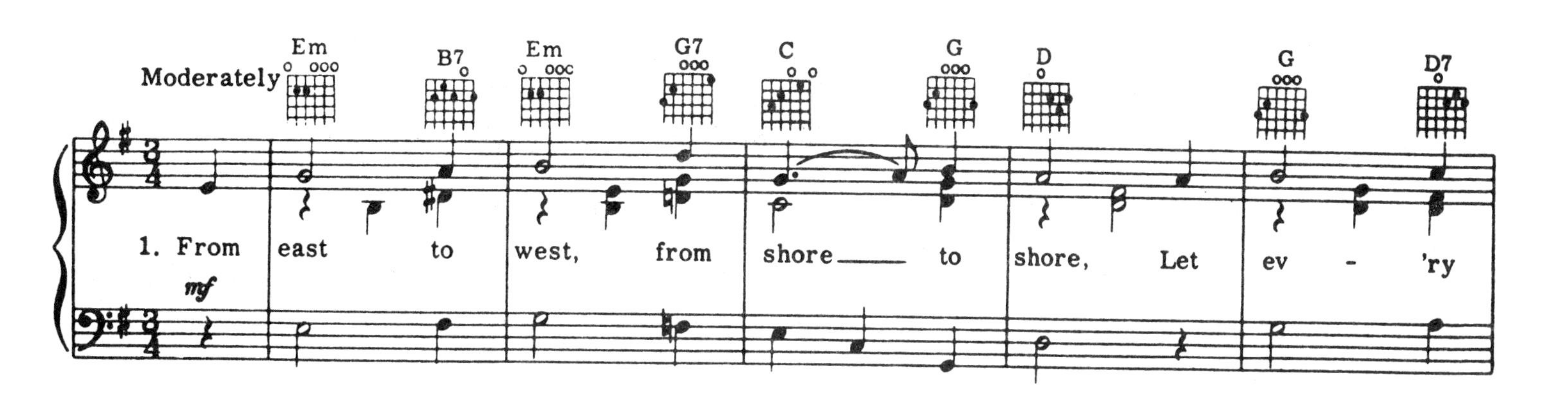
Moderately
Em
B7
Em
G7
C
G
D
G
D7
mf
1. From east to west, from shore to shore, Let ev - 'ry

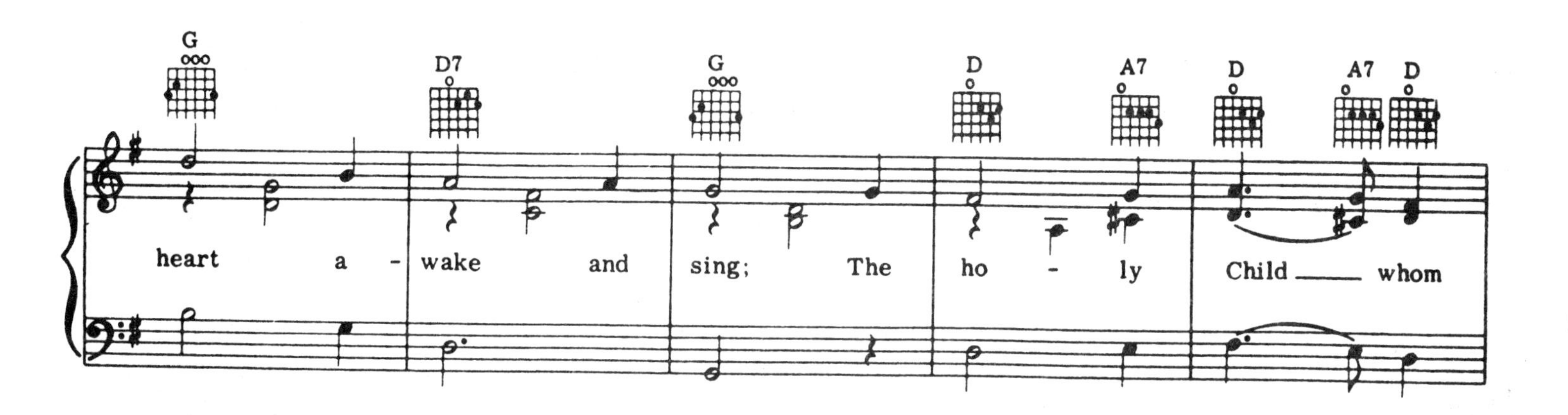
G
D7
G
D
A7
D
A7
D
heart a - wake and sing; The ho - ly Child whom

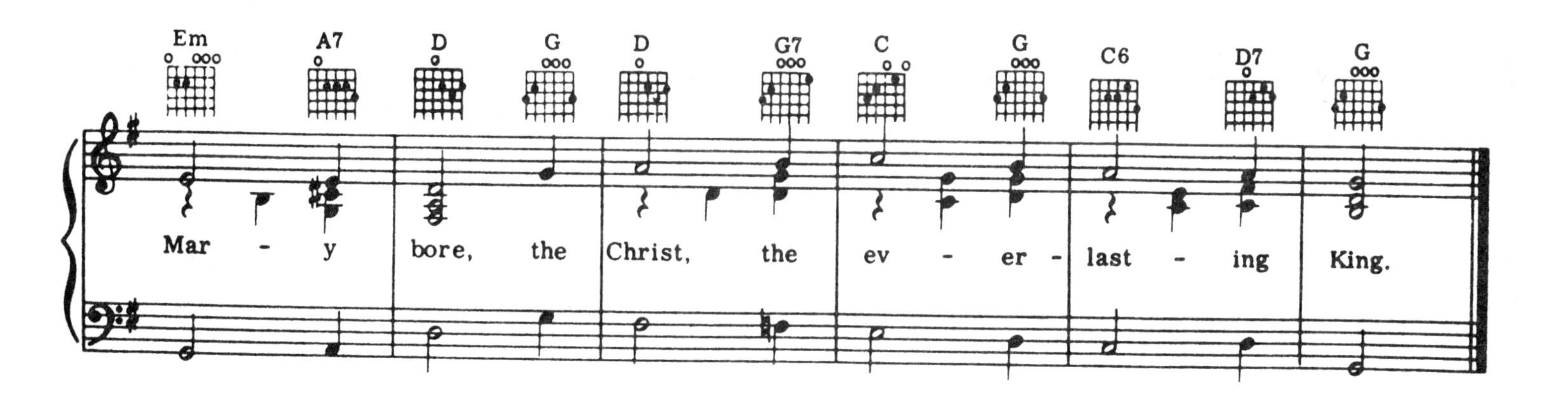
Em
A7
D
G
D
G7
C
G
C6
D7
G
Mar - y bore, the Christ, the ev - er - last - ing King.

2. Behold, the world's Creator wears
The form and fashion of a slave;
Our very flesh our Maker shares,
His fallen creature, man, to save.

3. For this how wondrously He wrought!
A maiden, in her lowly place,
Became, in ways beyond all thought,
The chosen vessel of His grace.

4. And while the angels in the sky
Sang praise above the silent field;
To shepherds poor the Lord most high,
The one great Shepherd, was revealed.

5. All glory for this blessed morn
To God the Father ever be;
All praise to Thee, O Virgin-born
All praise, O Holy Ghost, to Thee.

© 1970 (Assigned) WB MUSIC CORP. (ASCAP)
All Rights Administered by WARNER BROS. PUBLICATIONS U.S. INC.
All Rights Reserved including Public Performance for Profit

GESU BAMBINO
(The Infant Jesus)

Words by
FREDERICK H. MARTENS

Music by
PIETRO A. YON

* In bars 3-6 and where passage is repeated the melody in the accompaniment may be played on chimes. The introduction may be treated in like manner.

© 1917 J. FISCHER & BRO. (Renewed)
All Rights Assigned to and Controlled by BELWIN-MILLS PUBLISHING CORP. (ASCAP)
This Arrangement © 1970 BELWIN-MILLS PUBLISHING CORP.
All Rights Reserved including Public Performance for Profit

an - gels sang, the shep-herds sang, The grate - ful earth re - joiced,
And at His bless - ed birth the stars Their ex - ul - ta - tion
voiced. O come let us a -
Non troppo lento
sentito
dore Him, O come let us a - dore Him, O

rall.
a tempo
come let us a - dore Him, Christ the
rall.
a tempo
Lord.
A -
Tempo I
gain the heart with rap - ture glows To greet the ho - ly night That

a tempo
rall
gave_ the world_ its Christ-mas Rose, Its King_ of Love_ and Light. ___ Let
rall.
a tempo
p
ev - 'ry voice_ ac-claim His name, The grate-ful cho - rus swell, ___
p
f
___ From par - a-dise_ to earth He came That we_ with Him might
f
f

Non troppo lento
pp
dwell. O come let us a - dore Him, O come let us a - dore Him, O come let us a - dore Him Christ the Lord. Ah!
pp
rall.
a tempo
rall.
a tempo

O come let us a-dore Him,
a - dore Him Christ the Lord. O come, O
f
p
come, O come let us a - dore Him,
let us a - dore Him. Christ the Lord.
pp
rall.
a tempo
pp a tempo

GOD REST YE MERRY, GENTLEMEN

Traditional English Carol

© 1991 (Asssigned) WARNER BROS. PUBLICATIONS INC.
All Rights Reserved including Public Performance for Profit

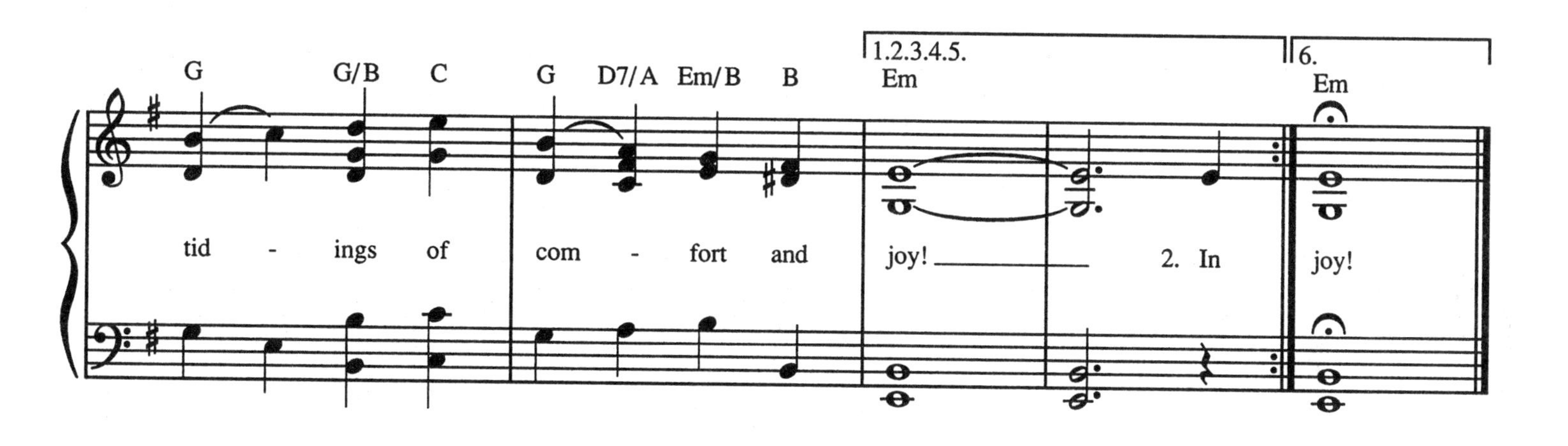

Verse 3:
From God, our Heav'nly Father,
A blessed Angel came,
And unto certain Shepherds
Brought tidings of the same;
How that in Bethlehem was born
The Son of God by Name.
(To Refrain:)

Verse 4:
"Fear not, then," said the Angel,
"Let nothing you affright,
This day is born a Saviour,
Of a pure Virgin bright,
To free all those who trust in Him
From Satan's power and might."
(To Refrain:)

Verse 5:
The Shepherds at those tidings
Rejoiced much in mind;
And left their flocks a-feeding,
In tempest, storm and wind;
And went to Bethlehem straight-way,
The Son of God to find.
(To Refrain:)

Verse 6:
Now to the Lord sing praises,
All you within this place,
And with true love and brotherhood
Each other now embrace;
This holy tide of Christmas
All other doth deface.
(To Refrain:)

GOOD CHRISTIAN MEN, REJOICE

Words by
JOHN MASON NEALE

Old German Carol

2. Good Christian men, rejoice
With heart and soul and voice,
Now ye hear of endless bliss;
Joy! Joy! Jesus Christ was born for this.
He hath ope'd the heav'nly door,
And man is blessed evermore;
Christ was born for this.
Christ was born for this.

3. Good Christian men, rejoice
With heart and soul and voice,
Now ye need not fear the grave:
Peace! Peace! Jesus Christ was born to save.
Calls you one and calls you all,
To gain His everlasting hall;
Christ was born to save.
Christ was born to save.

© 1965 (Renewed & Assigned) WARNER BROS. PUBLICATIONS INC.
All Rights Reserved including Public Performance for Profit

GOOD KING WENCESLAS

Words by
JOHN MASON NEALE

Traditional English Carol

Moderately
G Em D G C D C G C D7 G
mf
1. Good King Wen - ces - las looked out On the feast of Ste - phen,
Em D G C D C G C D7 G
When the snow lay 'round a - bout, Deep and crisp and e - ven.
Am G D G D Em C G C D7 G
Bright - ly shone the moon - that night, Though the frost was cru - el,
C D Em D G C G D7 Em C G
When a poor man came in sight, Gath - 'ring win - ter fu - el.

2. "Hither, page, and stand by me,
If thou know'st it telling,
Yonder peasant, who is he?
Where and what his dwelling?"
"Sire, he lives a good league hence,
Underneath the mountain,
Right against the forest fence,
By St. Agnes' fountain."

3. "Bring me flesh, and bring me wine,
Bring me pine logs hither;
Thou and I will see him dine,
When we bear them thither."
Page and monarch, forth they went,
Forth they went together;
Through the rude wind's wild lament,
And the bitter weather.

4. "Sire, the night is darker now,
And the wind blows stronger;
Fails my heart, I know not how;
I can go no longer."
"Mark my footsteps my good page,
Tread thou in them boldly:
Thou shalt find the winter's rage
Freeze thy blood less coldly."

5. In his master's steps he trod,
Where the snow lay dinted;
Heat was in the very sod
Which the Saint had printed.
Therefore, Christian men, be sure,
Wealth or rank possessing,
Ye who now will bless the poor,
Shall yourselves find blessing.

© 1965 (Renewed & Assigned) WARNER BROS. PUBLICATIONS INC.
All Rights Reserved including Public Performance for Profit

NOËL, NOËL

French-English
Arranged by SIR JOHN STAINER

Cantabile
mf
D G C G C G D C Bm C Am
1. 'Tis the day, the bless - ed day, On which our Lord was
2. In a hum - ble feed - ing trough, With - in a low - ly
3. He will save the per - ish - ing, Will waft the sighs to
B C G Am Am6 G C Am Em Am Em
born, And sweet - ly do the sun - beams gild The dew be - span - gled
shed, With cat - tle at His in - fant feet, And shep - herds at His
heav'n, Of guilt - y men, who tru - ly seek, And weep to be for -
D C G Am G D Em Bm C Am Em B
thorn. The birds sing through the heav - ens clear, The breez - es gent - ly
head, The Sav - ior of this sin - ful world In in - no - cence first
giv'n And In - ter - ces - sor still He shines, And men to Him should
Em C G Am Am6 G C Am Em Am Em D
play, And song and sun - shine love - ly, Be - gin this Ho - ly Day.
lay, And wise men made their off - 'ring, Up - on a Ho - ly Day.
pray, Be - fore His al - tar meek - ly, Up - on this Ho - ly Day.

© 1958 WARNER BROS. INC. (Renewed)
All Rights Reserved

REFRAIN
D Am Em G C Am D7 G Am
ff
No - ël, No - ël, No - ël, No - ël, No - ël, No - ël, No -
B C G Am D G Am Dm6 Am Em Am
ël, Now hear the sal - u - ta - tion Of an - gel Ga - bri - el.

GRANDMA GOT RUN OVER BY A REINDEER!

Words and Music by
RANDY BROOKS

© 1979 KRIS PUBLISHING INC. and ELMO PUBLISHING (SESAC)
All Rights Reserved

To Coda
B
E
D
A
as for me and Grand - pa, we be - lieve.
Verse:
E
B
1. She'd been drink - ing too much egg - nog
mp
E
and we begged her not to go,
E7
A
but she for - got her med - i - ca - tion, and she

B
E
stag - gered out the door in - to the snow.
C♯m
G♯m
When we found her Christ - mas morn - ing
B7
E
at the scene of the at - tack,
E7
A
she had hoof - prints on her fore - head, and in -

B
E
1st and 2nd time D.S.
3rd time D.S. al Coda
crim - i - nat - ing Claus marks on her back.
Coda
E
C♯
F♯
lieve.
Grand-ma got run o - ver by a
rein - deer
walk - ing home from our house Christ - mas
B
Eve.
You can say there's no such thing as

F♯
C♯
San - ta,
but as for me and Grand - pa, we be -
F♯
C♯
F♯
lieve.

Verse 2:
Now we're all so proud of Grandpa,
He's been taking this so well.
See him in there watching football,
Drinking beer and playing cards with Cousin Mel.
It's not Christmas without Grandma.
All the family's dressed in black,
And we just can't help but wonder:
Should we open up her gifts or send them back?

(To Chorus:)

Verse 3:
Now the goose is on the table,
And the pudding made of fig,
And the blue and silver candles,
That would just have matched the hair in Grandma's wig.
I've warned all my friends and neighbors,
Better watch out for yourselves.
They should never give a license
To a man who drives a sleigh and plays with elves.

(To Chorus:)

THE HAPPY CHRISTMAS COMES ONCE MORE

Words by
NICOLAI F.S. GRUNDTVIG
and C.P. KRAUTH

Music by
C. BALLE

Allegretto
D
A7
A
Bm
G6
mf
1. The happy Christmas comes once more, The heav'nly Guest is at the door, The blessed words, the shepherds thrill, The joyous tidings, peace, good-will.

2. To David's city let us fly,
Where angels sing beneath the sky,
Through plain and village pressing near,
And news from God with shepherds hear.

3. O, let us go with quiet mind,
The gentle Babe with shepherds find,
To gaze on Him who gladdens them,
The loveliest flow'r on Jesse's stem.

4. Come, Jesus, glorious heav'nly guest,
Keep Thine own Christmas in our breast;
Then David's harp-string, hushed so long,
Shall swell our jubilee of song.

© 1969 (Assigned) WB MUSIC CORP. (ASCAP)
All Rights Administered by WARNER BROS. PUBLICATIONS U.S. INC.
All Rights Reserved including Public Performance for Profit

HARK! THE BELLS ARE RINGING

Traditional

© 1965 (Renewed 1993) WB MUSIC CORP. (ASCAP)
All Rights Administered by WARNER BROS. PUBLICATIONS U.S. INC.
All Rights Reserved including Public Performance for Profit

HARK! THE HERALD ANGELS SING

Words and Music by
FELIX MENDELSSOHN
and CHAS. WESLEY

Moderato
f

G
D
G
Bm
Am
G
D
G
1. Hark! the her - ald an - gels sing, "Glo - ry to the new - born king!
3. Hail the heav'n born Prince of Peace! Hail the Sun of right - eous - ness!
mp

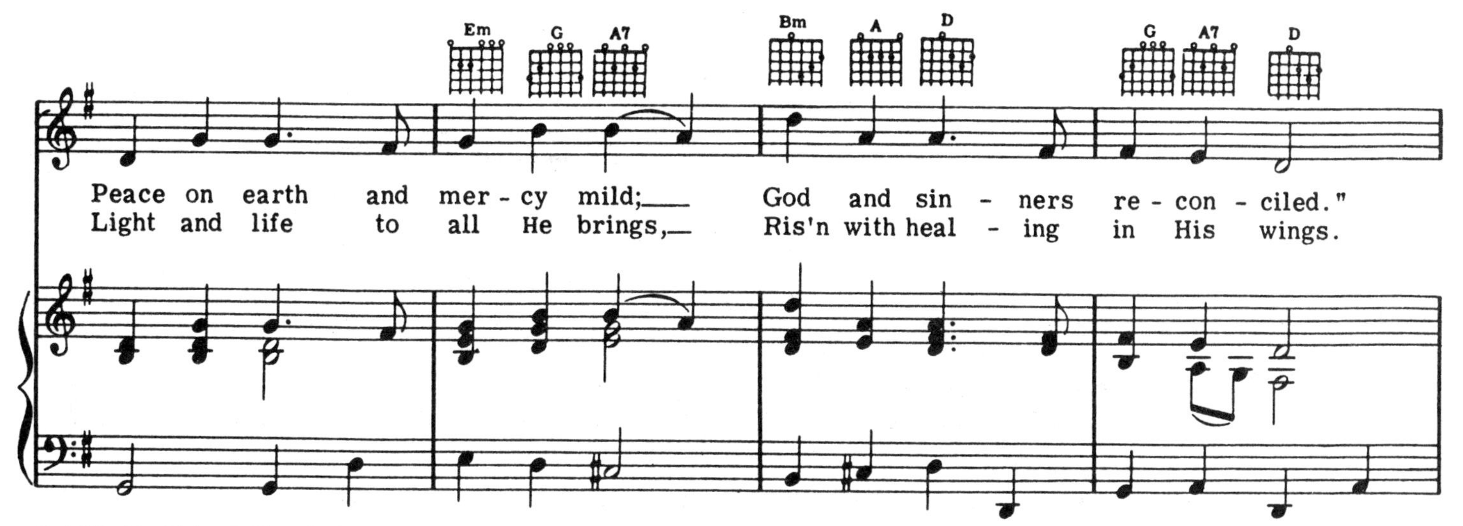
Em
G
A7
Bm
A
D
G
A7
D
Peace on earth and mer - cy mild; God and sin - ners re - con - ciled."
Light and life to all He brings, Ris'n with heal - ing in His wings.

© 1977 (Assigned) WARNER BROS. PUBLICATIONS INC.
All Rights Reserved including Public Performance for Profit

G D7 G D G D7 G D
Joy - ful, all ye na - tions rise, Join the tri - umph of the skies.
Mild, He lays His glo - ry by, Born that man no more may die,
mf
C G Am E Am D7 G D7 G
With an - gel - ic host pro - claim "Christ is born in Beth - le - hem."
Born to raise the sons of earth, Born to give them sec - ond birth.
f
C G Am E Am D D7 G D G
Fine
Hark! the her - ald an - gels sing, "Glo - ry to the new born king!"
Hark! the her - ald an - gels sing, "Glo - ry to the new born king!"
rit. last time
G D G Bm Am G D G
2. Christ, by high - est heav'n a - dored, Christ the ev - er - last - ing Lord,
mp lightly

Em G Em A7 Bm A D Bm A7 D
Late in time be - hold Him come, Off - spring of the Vir - gin's womb.
G D7 G D G D7 G D
Veiled in flesh she God - head see, Hail th' in - car - nate De - i - ty.
mf
C G Am E Am D7 G D7 G
Pleased as man with men ap - pear, Je - sus, our Im - man - uel here.
f
C G Am E Am D D7 G D7 G
D.S. al Fine
Hark! the her - ald an - gels sing, "Glo - ry to the new - born king!"

HAVE YOURSELF A MERRY LITTLE CHRISTMAS

Words and Music by
HUGH MARTIN and
RALPH BLANE

© 1943 (Renewed 1971) METRO-GOLDWYN-MAYER INC.
© 1944 (Renewed 1972) EMI FEIST CATALOG INC.
All Rights Controlled by EMI FEIST CATALOG INC. (Publishing) and WARNER BROS. PUBLICATIONS INC. (Print)
All Rights Reserved

C Am7 Dm7 G7 E7 A7 D9 G7
From now on, our trou-bles will be out of sight.
C Dm7 Dm7/G G7 C Dm7/G G7
Have your - self a mer - ry lit - tle Christ - mas, make the yule - tide gay.
C Am7 Dm7 E7 Am C7 C7(♭9) C7(♭9 ♯5)
From now on, our trou-bles will be miles a - way.
F(9) Fm C/E E♭dim Dm7 Dm7/G G+ Cmaj7 Am7
Here we are as in old - en days, hap - py gold - en days of yore.

F♯m7(♭5) B13(♭9) B7(♭13) Em A7(♭5) G/D Am7/D D7 Dm7/G G7
Faith - ful friends who are dear to us, gath - er near to us once more.
C Dm7 Dm7/G G7 C Dm7/G G7
Through the years we all will be to - geth - er, if the Fates al - low.
C Am7 Dm7 E7(♭9) Am C7 C7(♭9) C7(♯5)
Hang a shin - ing star up - on the high - est bough, and
F Am/E Dm7 Dm7/G G7(♭9) C Am Dm G7 C Dm7 Cmaj7
1.
2.
have your-self a mer-ry lit-tle Christ-mas now. now.
mf
rall.
p

HERE COMES SANTA CLAUS
(Right Down Santa Claus Lane)

Words and Music by
GENE AUTRY and
OAKLEY HALDEMAN

Moderately bright
F
C7
Cdim
C7
1. 2. 3. 4. Here comes San-ta Claus! Here comes San-ta Claus! Right down San-ta Claus Lane!
mp
F
Fdim
F
F7
Vix - en and Blitz - en and all his rein - deer are pull - ing on the rein.
He's got a bag that is filled with toys for the boys and girls a - gain.
He does-n't care if you're rich or poor for he loves you just the same.
He'll come a-round when the chimes ring out, then it's Christ-mas morn a - gain.
Bb
Bdim
F
D7
Gm7
C7
F
F7
3
Bells are ring - ing, chil - dren sing - ing, all is mer - ry and bright.
Hear those sleigh bells jin - gle jan - gle, what a beau - ti - ful sight.
San - ta knows that we're God's chil - dren, that makes ev - 'ry - thing right.
Peace on earth will come to all if we just fol - low the light.
mf
Bb
Bdim
F
D7
Gm
C7
1. 2. 3.
F
4.
F
Hang your stock - ings and say your pray'rs, 'Cause San-ta Claus comes to- night.
Jump in bed, cov - er up your head, 'Cause San-ta Claus comes to- night.
Fill your hearts with a Christ-mas cheer, 'Cause San-ta Claus comes to- night.
Let's give thanks to the Lord a - bove, 'Cause San-ta Claus comes to- night.

© 1947 (Renewed 1975) WESTERN MUSIC PUBLISHING CO.
All Rights Reserved

HE'S GOT THE WHOLE WORLD IN HIS HANDS

Traditional Spiritual

Moderately
F
C7
mf
1. He's got the whole world in His hands; He's got the whole wide world in His hands; He's got the whole world in His hands; He's got the whole world in His hands. He's got the
earth and sky in His hands; He's got the night and day in His hands; He's got the sun and moon in His hands; He's got the

© 1968 (Assigned) WB MUSIC CORP. (ASCAP)
All Rights Administered by WARNER BROS. PUBLICATIONS U.S. INC.
All Rights Reserved including Public Performance for Profit

C7
1. 2.
F
3.
whole world in His hands. He's got the hands. He's got the
whole world — in His hands; — He's got the whole wide world —
in His hands; — He's got the whole world — in His hands; — He's got the
whole world in His hands. —

2. He's got the whole world in His hands;
He's got the whole wide world in His hands;
He's got the whole world in His hands;
He's got the whole world in His hands.
He's got the land and sea in His hands;
He's got the wind and rain in His hands;
He's got the spring and fall in His hands;
He's got the whole world in His hands.

3. He's got the whole world in His hands;
He's got the whole wide world in His hands;
He's got the whole world in His hands;
He's got the whole world in His hands.
He's got the young and old in His hands;
He's got the rich and poor in His hands;
Yes, He's got ev'ry one in His hands;
He's got the whole world in His hands.

HOLIDAY TIME IS NEAR

Words and Music by
LEONARD C. CHRISTMAN

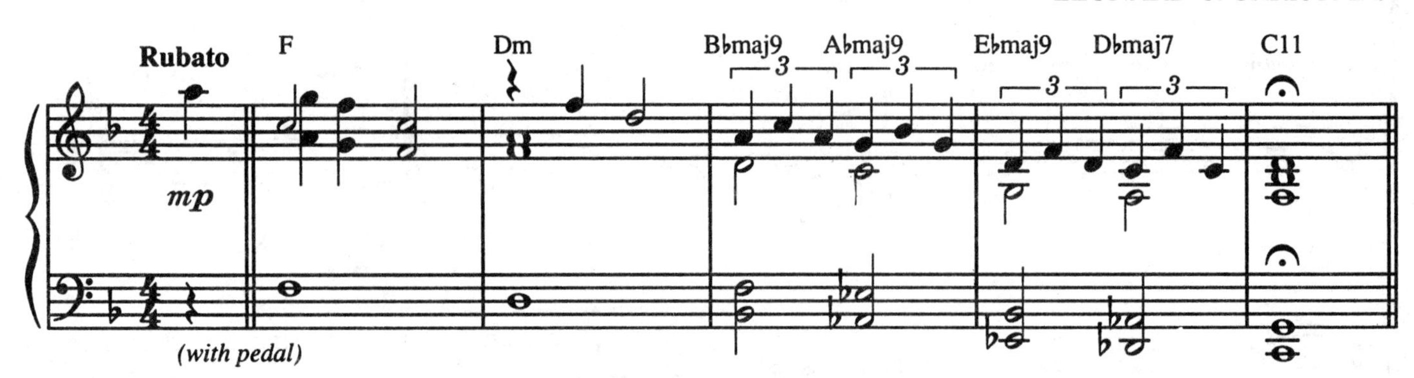

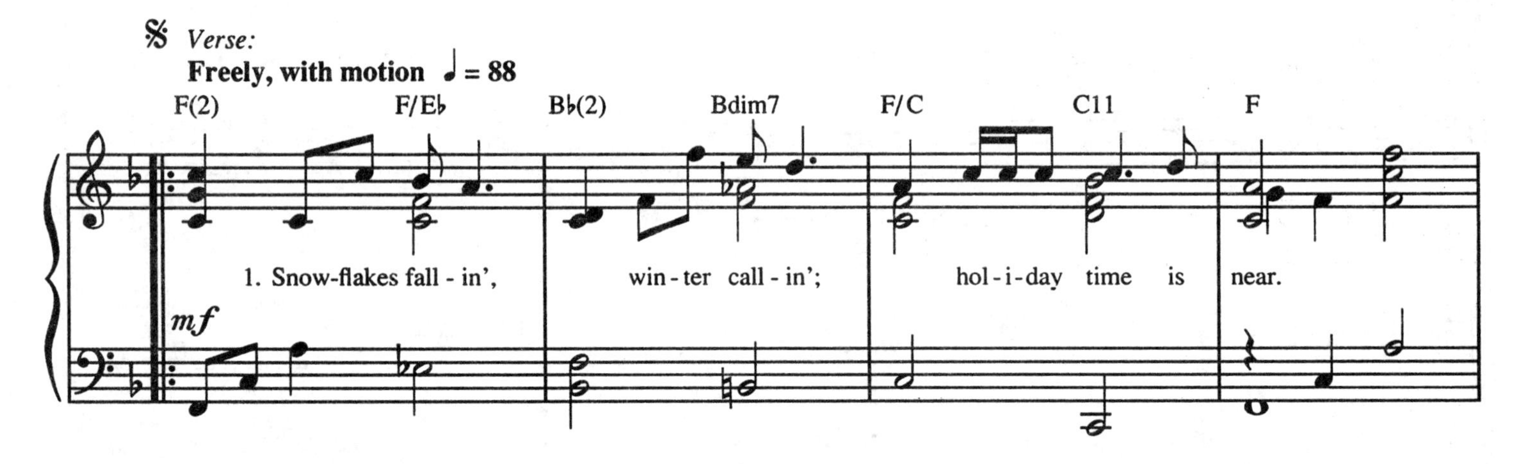

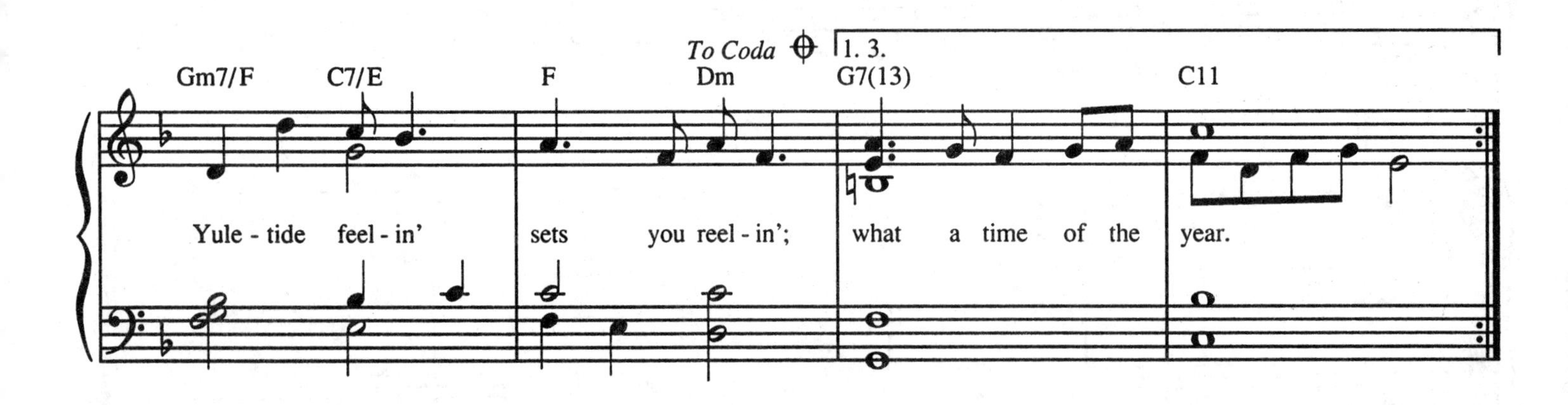

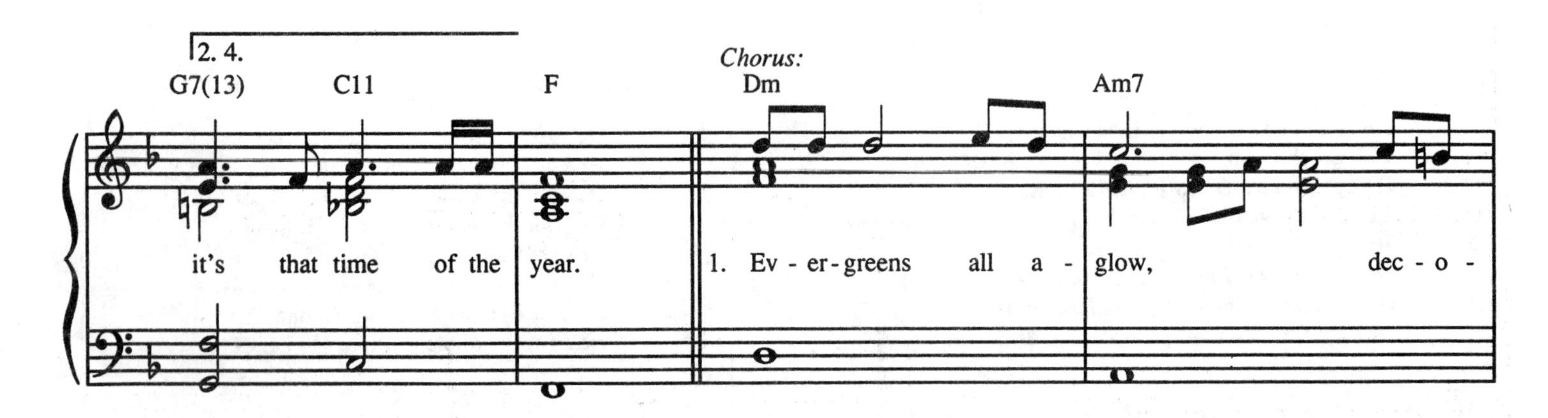

Copyright © 1993 by SONGCASTLE MUSIC (ASCAP)
This arrangement © 1993 by SONGCASTLE MUSIC Administered by COPYRIGHT MANAGEMENT, INC.
International Copyright Secured Made in U.S.A. All Rights Reserved

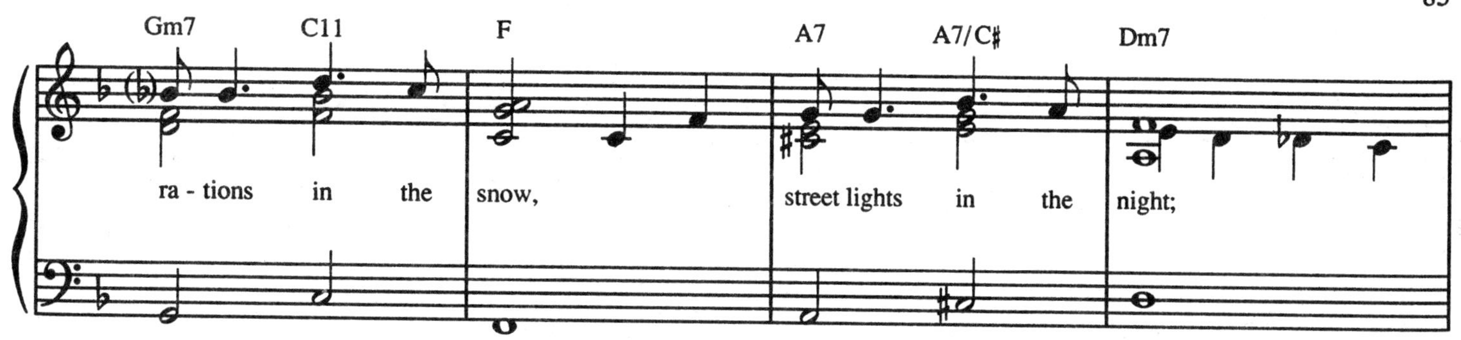
Gm7
C11
F
A7
A7/C♯
Dm7
ra - tions in the snow,
street lights in the night;

G9
1.
D.S. 𝄋
2.
D.S. 𝄋 al Coda
C7
C7
oh, what a won - der - ful
sight. 3. And the time is ripe for...
Day. And I love the sound of...

Coda
G7(13)
C11
F
Gm
D7
Gm
ring - ing in the New
Year. It's
time to sing, it's

B♭
time to swing, 'cause
hol - i - day time,
hap - py

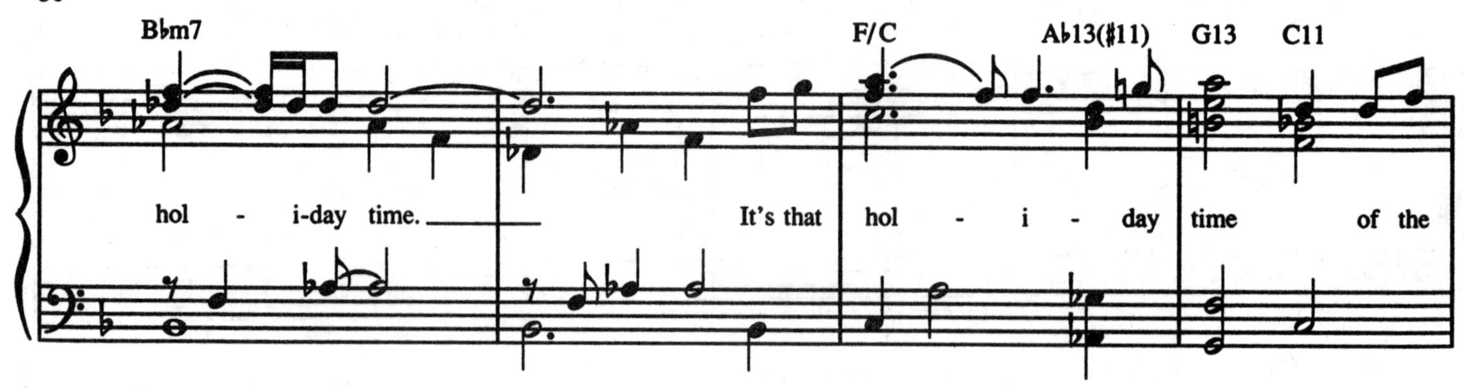

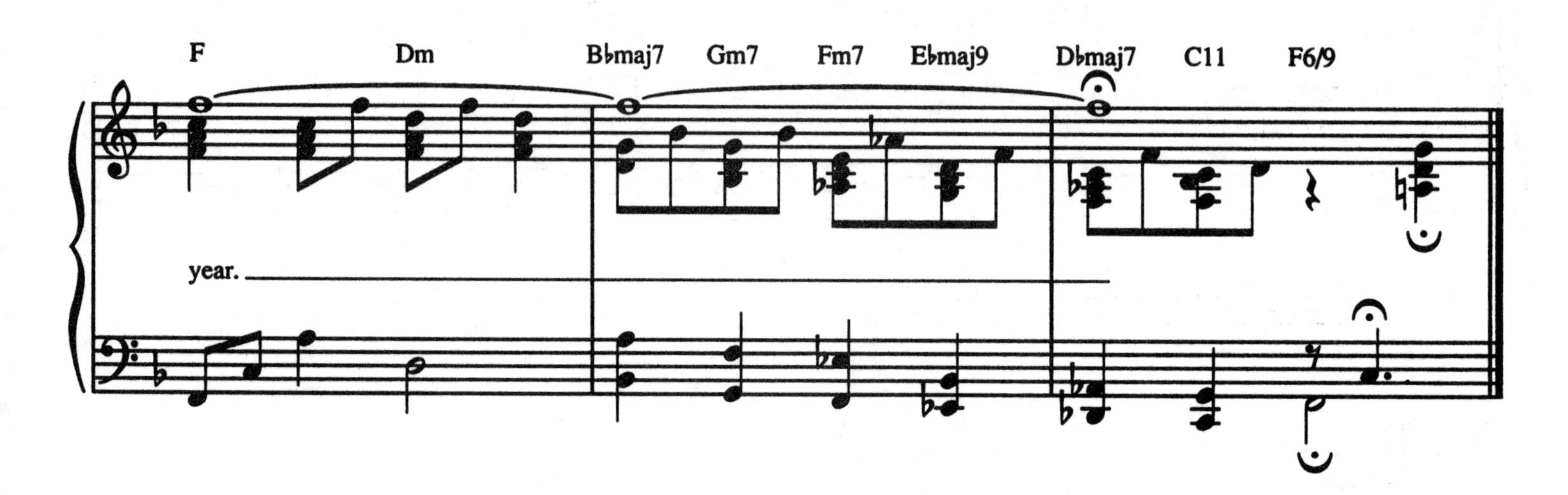

Verse 2:
Window shoppin', toy store hoppin'; holiday time is near.
Popcorn stringin', carol singin'; it's that time of the year.
(To Chorus 1:)

Verse 3:
Candy makin', cookie bakin'; holiday time is near.
Chestnut roastin', family toastin', what a time of the year.

Verse 4:
Children dreamin', faces beamin'; holiday time is near.
Present wrappin' while they're nappin'; it's that time of the year.

Chorus 2:
Sleigh rides in the snow, holly wreaths and mistletoe,
Santa's on his way; soon it will be Christmas Day.
And I love the sound of...

Verse 5:
People greetin' when they're meetin', sharin' their Christmas cheer.
Congregatin', celebratin'; ringin' in the New Year.
(To Coda)

I WANT AN OLD-FASHIONED CHRISTMAS

By FLORENCE TARR
and FAY FOSTER

© 1945 (Renewed 1973) EMI ROBBINS CATALOG INC.
All Rights Administered by EMI ROBBINS CATALOG INC. (Publishing)
and WARNER BROS. PUBLICATIONS INC. (Print)
All Rights Reserved

C
G7
C
Am
Dm7
C
G7
C
home - folks cheer - i - ly nod - ding a mer - ry warm "Hel - lo!"
Eb7
Ab
4 fr.
Bbm7
I want to hear the lit - tle
Db
Ab
4 fr.
Db
Dbm
Ab
4 fr.
Ab6
D7-5
chil - dren sing - ing the Christ - mas car - ols I used to know; And
C
G7
C
G7
Am7
hear the ev - 'ning church - bells ring - ing out their joy - ous wel - come of

Dm7 G7 C Dm E7 C G7
long a - go. I want an old - fash - ioned
rit. a tempo
C C7 F G7
Christ - mas, To be a child a - gain, To make be - lieve that there's a
C A7 Fm6 G7 C G7 C G7
San - ta, For I was hap - pi - est then. Mer - ry Christ - mas! Mer - ry
F+ A7 Dm7 C
Christ - mas! Mer - ry Christ - mas!
rit.

From the Videocraft T.V. Musical Spectacular "RUDOLPH, THE RED-NOSED REINDEER"

A HOLLY JOLLY CHRISTMAS

By JOHNNY MARKS

Moderately Bright With A Happy Feeling

© 1962 (Renewed 1990) ST. NICHOLAS MUSIC, INC.
This Arrangement © 1964 (Renewed 1992) ST. NICHOLAS MUSIC, INC.
All Rights Reserved Used by Permission

C F Em F
meet. Oh, ho, the mis - tle - toe hung where you can
mf
dim. poco a poco
C Dm Am D7 Am7 D7
see. Some - bod - y waits for you, kiss her once for
p
G7 C C♯dim
me. Have A HOL - LY JOL - LY CHRIST-MAS, and in case you did - n't hear
G7 C 1. D7 G7
Oh, by gol - ly, have A HOL - LY JOL - LY CHRIST - MAS this
mf
C G7 2. D7 G7 C Dm7 G7 C
year. Have A CHRIST - MAS this year.
mp
mf
f

(There's No Place Like)

HOME FOR THE HOLIDAYS

Words by
AL STILLMAN

Music by
ROBERT ALLEN

© 1954 RONCOM MUSIC CO.
Copyright Renewed 1982 and Assigned to CHARLIE DEITCHER PRODUCTIONS INC. and KITTY ANNE MUSIC CO., INC.
This Arrangement © 1969 CHARLIE DEITCHER PRODUCTIONS INC. and KITTY ANNE MUSIC CO., INC.
All Rights Reserved

F
F♯dim
C
C♯dim
man who lives in Ten - nes - see and he was head - in' for Penn - syl -
G7
F♯7
G7
C
C7
Gm7
C7
van - ia and some home - made pump - kin pie. From Penn - syl -
F
F♯dim
C
Cm
van - ia folks are trav - 'lin' down to Dix - ie's sun - ny shore; From At -
G
G♯dim
Am7
D7
G7
C♯dim
Dm7
G7
D. S. al Coda
lan - tic to Pa - cif - ic, gee, the traf - fic is ter - rif - ic. Oh, there's
Coda
G7
C♯dim
Dm7
G9
G7-9
C
F6
C
can't beat home, sweet home.
cresc.
f

I WONDER AS I WANDER

Words and Music by
JOHN JACOB NILES

2. When Jesus was born, it was in a cow's stall,
With shepherds and wise men and angels and all.
The blessings of Christmas from heaven did fall,
And the weary world woke to the Savior's call.

© 1969 (Assigned) WB MUSIC CORP. (ASCAP)
All Rights Administered by WARNER BROS. PUBLICATIONS U.S. INC.
All Rights Reserved including Public Performance for Profit

I'D LIKE TO TEACH THE WORLD TO SING
(In Perfect Harmony)

Words and Music by
B. BACKER, B. DAVIS,
R. COOK and R. GREENAWAY

© 1971, 1972 THE COCA-COLA COMPANY
Copyright Assigned to SHADA MUSIC, INC.
All Rights Reserved Used by Permission

C
Bb
like to hold it in my arms and keep it com - pa - ny.
F
I'd like to see the world for once all
G7
C
stand - ing hand in hand, And hear them ech - o through
Bb
F
Fine
the hills for peace through - out the land.
Fine

F
G7
That's the song I hear, let the world sing to - day.
C
Bb
F
A song of peace that ech-oes on and nev-er goes a-way. I'd
G7
like to build the world a home and fur-nish it with love, Grow
C
Bb
C7
D. S. al Fine
ap-ple trees and hon-ey bees and snow white tur-tle doves. I'd
D. S. al Fine

OH HAPPY DAY

Words and Music by
EDWIN R. HAWKINS

© 1969 KAMA-RIPPA MUSIC, INC. and EDWIN R. HAWKINS MUSIC CO.
All Rights Controlled by EMI U CATALOG INC. (Publishing) and WARNER BROS. PUBLICATIONS INC. (Print)
All Rights Reserved

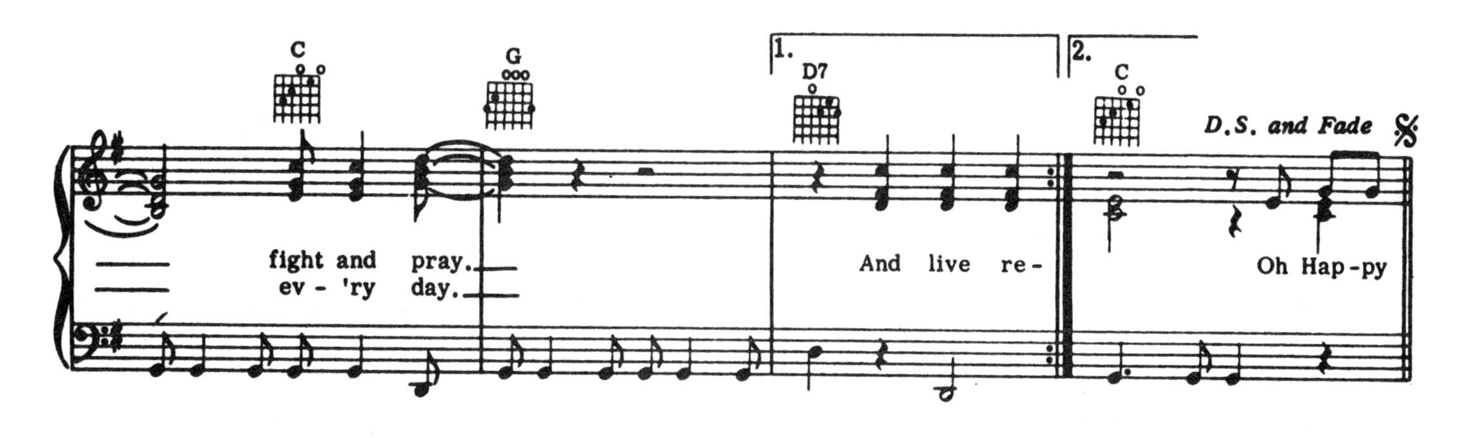
C
G
1.
D7
2.
C
D.S. and Fade
fight and pray.
ev - 'ry day.
And live re-
Oh Hap-py

I'LL BE HOME FOR CHRISTMAS

Words by
KIM GANNON

Music by
WALTER KENT

© 1943 (Renewed) GANNON & KENT MUSIC CO., INC.
All Rights Reserved

IN A CHRISTMAS MOOD

Lyric by
JUDY SPENCER

Music by
EARL ROSE

*Melody sung one octave lower

Copyright © 1993 by AMADEUS MUSIC CO. and WRITTEN WORD MUSIC CO. (ASCAP)
International Copyright Secured Made in U.S.A. All Rights Reserved

Em7
A7
D7sus
D7
G(9)
Am7
Bm7
Am7
Christ - mas mood. Just the thought of can - dy canes
Gmaj7
G♯dim7
Am7
D7
Gmaj7
E13
Am7
D9
framed in frost - ed win-dow panes while the car - ols all be - gin. Now,
Am7
Bm7
E9
A13
D7sus
G(9)
how could I help be - ing in a Christ - mas mood? With
C(9)
D7
G(9)
Am7
D7
G(9)
shop - pers fill - ing down - town stores and toy shelves al - most cleared, with

C♯m7 F♯7 Bm7 E7 D7 A♯dim7 Am7 D7
young-sters sit-ting on San - ta's lap, tell - ing him se-crets and rum-pling his beard. The
G(9) Am7 Bm7 Am7 Gmaj7 G♯dim7 Am7 D7
light - ed trees and fall - ing snow, cards from ev - 'ry - one I know, a
Gmaj7 E13 Am7 D7 Bm7 E9
kitch - en full of friends and par - ty food. No
Am7 D7sus D7 G(9)
won - der that I'm in a Christ - mas mood!
rit.
pp

I HEARD THE BELLS ON CHRISTMAS DAY

Words by
HENRY WADSWORTH LONGFELLOW
(Adapted by JOHNNY MARKS)

Music by
JOHNNY MARKS

© 1956 (Renewed 1984) ST. NICHOLAS MUSIC, INC.
All Rights Reserved Used by Permission

Dm6 (F Bass) C7 F F7 B♭ C7
Will To Men. I thought, as now this day had come, The
Will To Men." Then pealed the bells more loud and deep, "God
Dm Dm6 F E7 Am Gm C7
bel - fries of all Chris - ten - dom Had rung so long the un-
is not dead, nor doth He sleep, The wrong shall fail, The
Am7-5 D7 1. Gm D7 Gm Dm6 Gm7 C7 F
bro - ken song Of Peace On Earth, Good Will To Men.
right pre - vail, With
2. Gm D7 Gm Dm6 Gm7 C7 F
Peace On Earth, Good Will To Men."
8va
rit.

IT'S THE MOST WONDERFUL TIME OF THE YEAR

By EDDIE POLA and GEORGE WYLE

Bright waltz tempo (Happily)
Eb Cm Fm7 Bb9
f
Voice
Eb Cm Fm7 Bb7 Eb Cm
It's the most won-der-ful time of the year.
hap - hap-pi-est sea - son of all.
Fm7 Bb7 Fm7 Bb7 Eb Eb7
With the kids jing-le bell-ing, and ev-'ry-one tell-ing you,
With those hol-i-day greet-ings, and gay hap-py meet-ings when
Ab Aþdim Eb Cm
"Be of good cheer," it's the most won-der-ful
friends come to call, it's the hap - hap-pi-est

© 1963 BARNABY MUSIC CORP. (Renewed)
All Rights Reserved Used by Permission

1.
2.
Fm7
B♭7
G♭
Fm7
B♭7
B♭m7
time of the year. It's the
sea - son of all.
E♭7
B♭m7
E♭7
A♭
A♮dim
E♭/B♭
Cm7
There'll be par-ties for host-ing, marsh-mal-lows for toast-ing and
Fm7
B♭7
E♭
E♭7
A♭m7
D♭7
car - ol - ing out in the snow. There'll be scar - y ghost sto - ries and
G♭maj7
E♭m
Fm7(♭5)
C♭7
Fm7/B♭
B♭7 Fm7
tales of the glo - ries of Christ-mas-es long long a - go.

B♭9
E♭
Cm
Fm7
B♭7
E♭
Cm
It's the most wonder-ful time of the year.
Fm7
B♭7
Fm7
B♭7
E♭
E♭7
There'll be much mis - tle - toe - ing and hearts will be glow - ing, when
A♭
A♮dim
E♭
loved ones are near.
It's the most
Cm7
Fm7
B♭7
E♭
C♭
A♭m
E♭
won-der - ful time of the year.

MERRY CHRISTMAS, DARLING

Lyric by FRANK POOLER

Music by RICHARD CARPENTER

Rubato
Cm7
Dm7
Gm7
Cm7
F7
B♭
Greet-ing cards have all been sent, the Christ-mas rush is through,

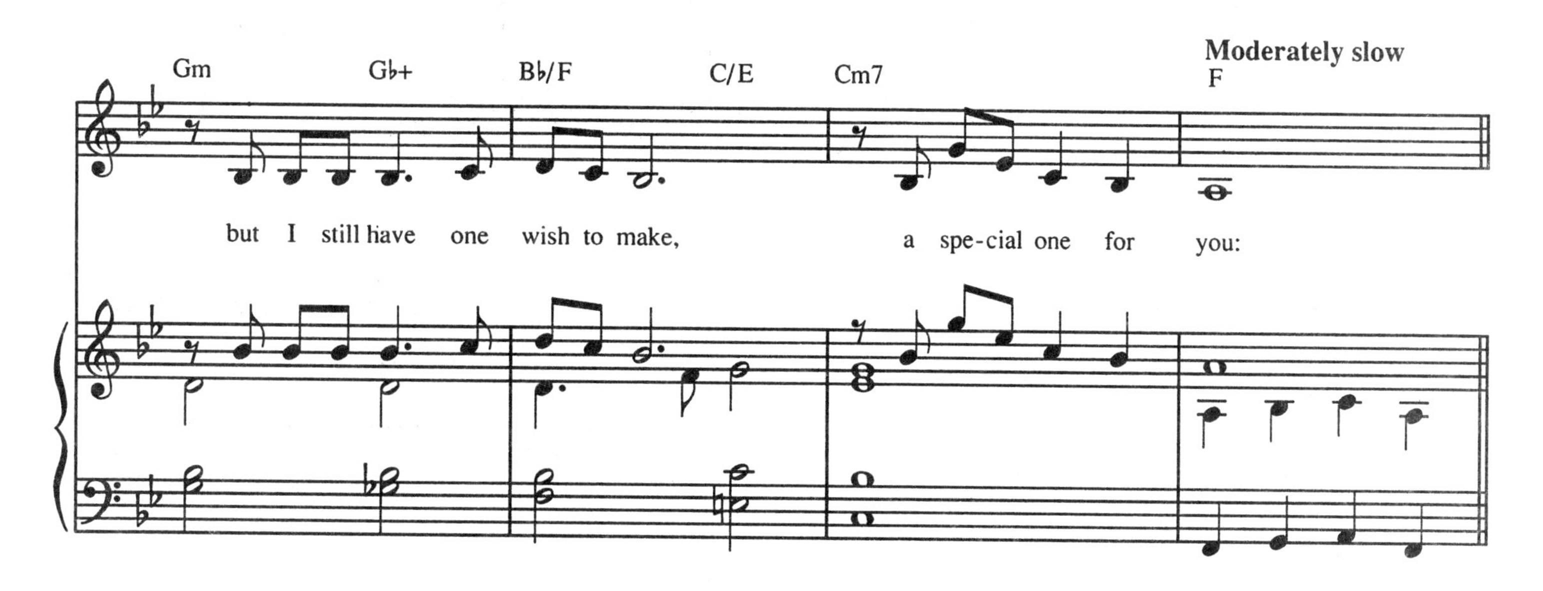
Gm
G♭+
B♭/F
C/E
Cm7
Moderately slow
F
but I still have one wish to make, a spe-cial one for you:

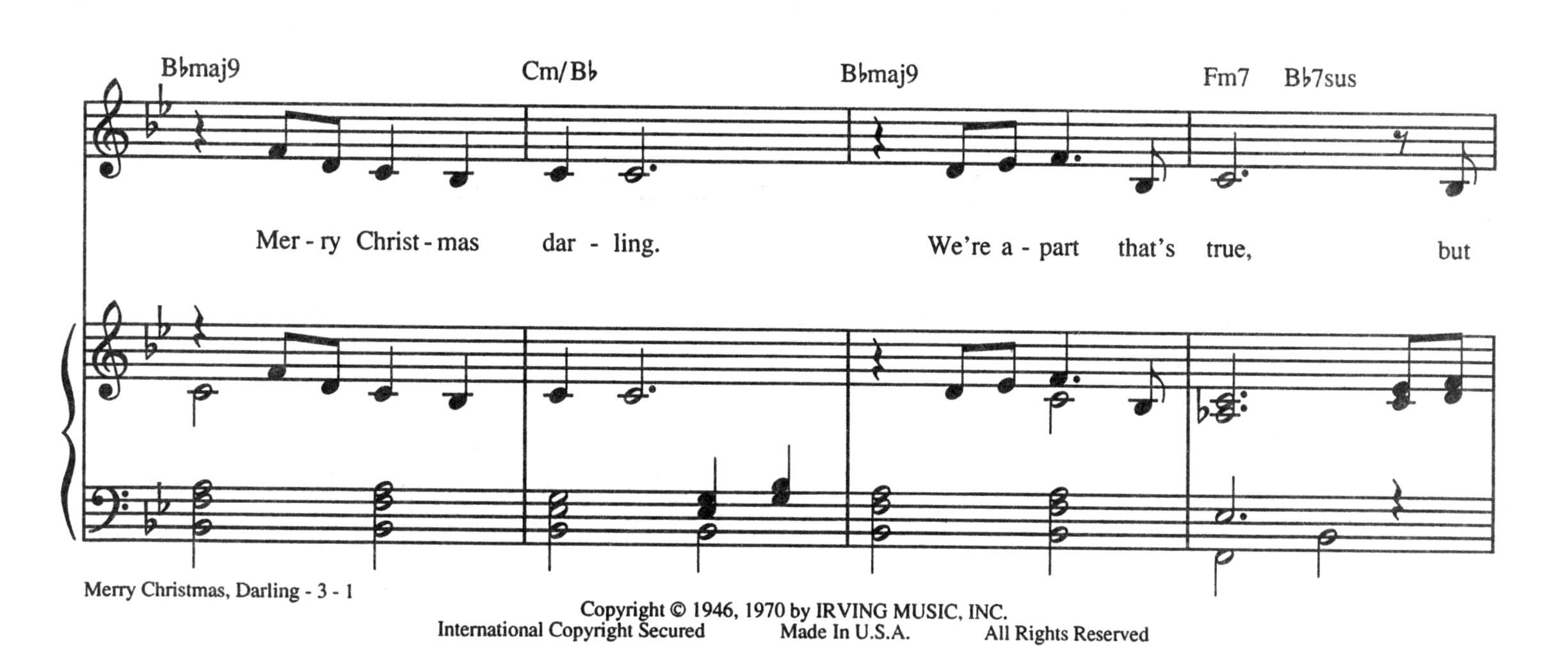
B♭maj9
Cm/B♭
B♭maj9
Fm7
B♭7sus
Mer-ry Christ-mas dar-ling. We're a-part that's true, but

Copyright © 1946, 1970 by IRVING MUSIC, INC.
International Copyright Secured Made In U.S.A. All Rights Reserved

Eb F/Eb Dm7 Gm7 Cm7 Dm Eb6 Eb/F F7
I can dream and in my dreams, I'm Christ - mas - ing with you.
Bbmaj9 Cm/Bb Bbmaj9 Fm7 Fm7/Bb
Hol - i - days are joy - ful. There's al - ways some - thing new. But
Eb F/Eb Dm7 Gm7 C/E Ebm6 Ab7
ev - 'ry - day's a hol - i - day when I'm near to you. The
Db Eb/Db Cm7 Fm Bbm7 Eb7 Ab
lights on my tree, I wish you could see, I wish it ev - 'ry day. The

Fm
Fm(♯7)/E
Fm7/E♭
F9
B♭
Cm
Dm
Cm7
F
logs on the fire fill me with de - sire, to see you and to say; that I
B♭maj9
Cm/B♭
B♭maj9
Fm7
E7(♭5)
wish you Mer - ry Christ - mas, Hap - py New Year too; I've
E♭
F/E♭
Dm7
Gm7
1. Cm7
F7
B♭
A♭7
D.S. 𝄋
just one wish on this Christ-mas eve; I wish I were with you. The
2. Cm
F
E♭
Dm7(♭5)
G7
rit.
Cm7
F7
E♭/B♭
F/A
Gm
E♭/F
B♭maj9
I wish I were with you, I wish I were with you.

IT CAME UPON THE MIDNIGHT CLEAR

Words by
EDMUND H. SEARS

Music by
RICHARD S. WILLIS

© 1991 (Assigned) WARNER BROS. PUBLICATIONS INC.
All Rights Reserved including Public Performance for Profit

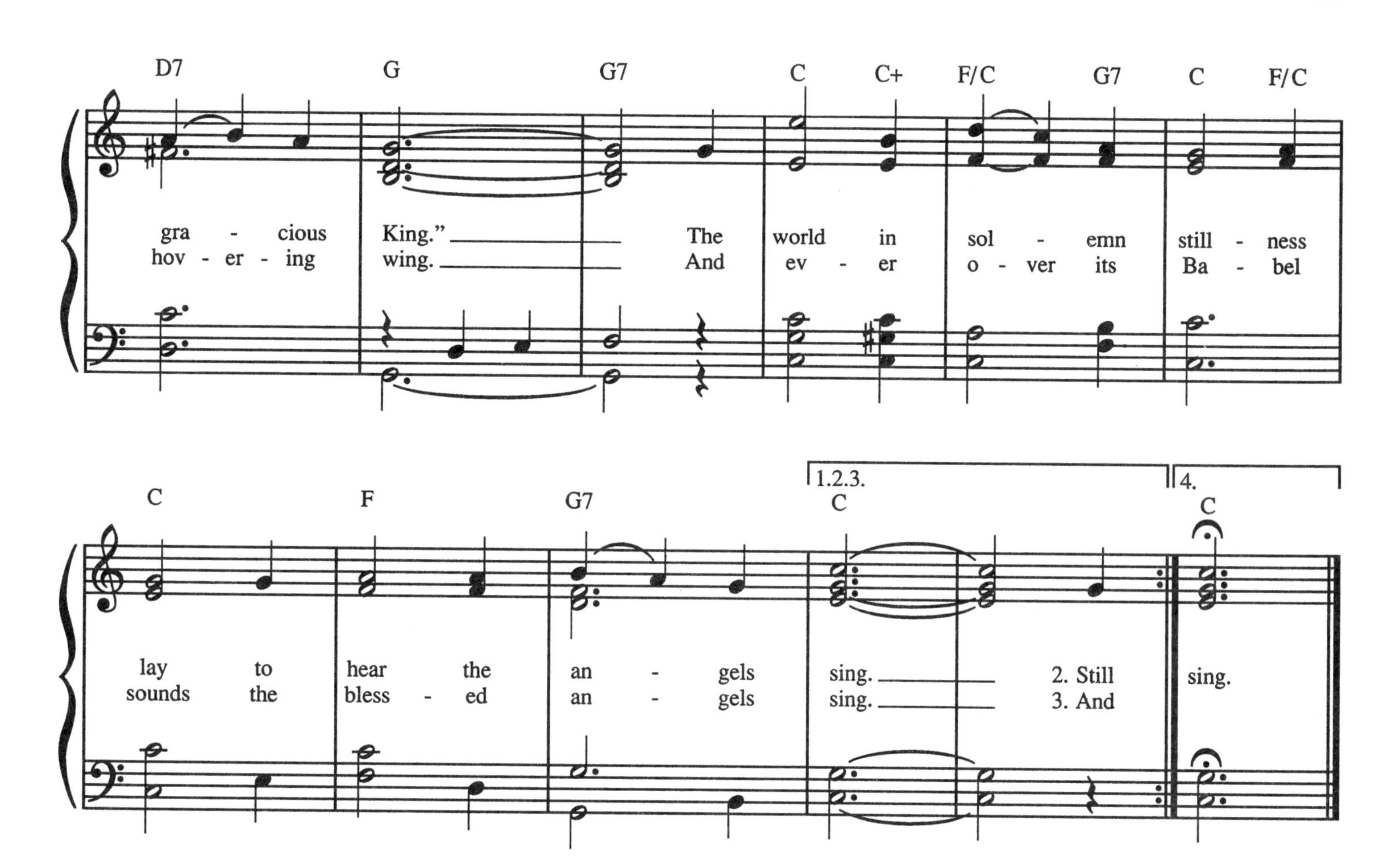

Verse 3:
And ye beneath life's crushing load,
Whose forms are bending low,
Who toil along the climbing way
With painful steps and slow,
Look now, for glad and golden hours
Come swiftly on the wing.
O rest beside the weary road
And hear the angels sing.

Verse 4:
For lo, the days are hast'ning on,
By prophets seen of old.
When, with the ever-circling years,
Shall come the time foretold,
When the new heav'n and earth shall own
The Prince of Peace, their King.
And the whole world send back the song,
Which now the angels sing.

JESU, JOY OF MAN'S DESIRING
(from Cantata No. 147)

English Text by BERNARD GASSO
JOHANN SEBASTIAN BACH
Slowly (♩=80)
mp
Je - su, joy of man's de - sir - ing, Thou whose love shines down like a guid - ing light; Drawn to Thee with souls as - pir - ing,
Je - su, joy of man's de - sir - ing, Lead us on with strains of a peace - ful song; With Thy wis - dom so in - spir - ing,
Through our faith we reach a ce - les - tial height. Son of God, we pray we may reach Thee! May we live in peace, we be - seech Thee!
Lead all men to love and to do no wrong. Son of God, we beg near - ly breath - less, May we know the peace which is death - less.
mf
f
O - pen doors of truth un - known, As Thy love comes

© 1972 (Assigned) WB MUSIC CORP. (ASCAP)
All Rights Administered by WARNER BROS. PUBLICATIONS U.S. INC.
All Rights Reserved including Public Performance for Profit

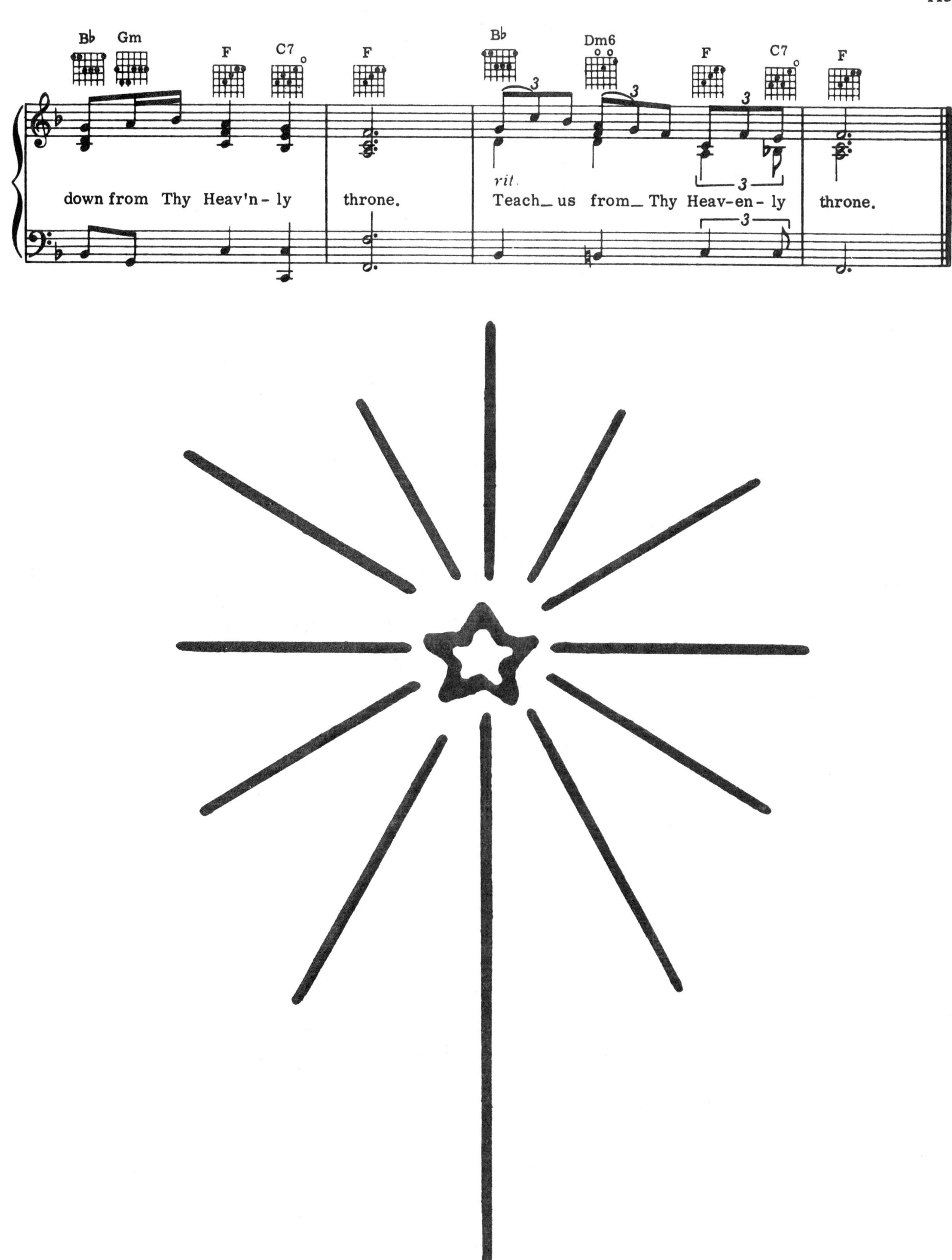
B♭ Gm F C7 F B♭ Dm6 F C7 F
down from Thy Heav'n - ly throne.
rit.
Teach_ us from_ Thy Heav-en - ly throne.

JOLLY OLD ST. NICHOLAS

© 1974 (Assigned) WARNER BROS. PUBLICATIONS INC.
All Rights Reserved including Public Performance for Profit

B♭
F7
Christ - mas Eve is com - ing soon;
All the stock - ings you will find
Now I think I'll leave to you
Gm
Dm
E♭
Now, my dear old man, Whis - per what you'll
Hang - ing in a row; Mine will be the
What to give the rest; Choose for me, dear
B♭
F7
B♭
bring to me, Tell me, if you can.
short - est one, You'll be sure to know.
San - ta Claus, You will know the best.

JOY TO THE WORLD

Words by
ISAAC WATTS
Music by
G.F. HANDEL
Moderate
D
Em
A7
G
1. Joy to the world! The Lord is come; Let earth receive her King; Let ev-'ry heart prepare Him
2. Joy to the world! The Savior reigns; Let men their songs employ; While field and floods, rocks, hills, and
3. He rules the world! With Truth and grace, And makes the nations prove The glories of His righteous-
mf
Joy to the World - 2 - 1

© 1974 (Assigned) WARNER BROS. PUBLICATIONS INC.
All Rights Reserved including Public Performance for Profit

room, And heav'n and na - ture sing, And
plains Re - peat the sound - ing joy, Re -
ness, And won - ders of His love, And
A
A7
D
G
heav'n and na - ture sing, And heav'n, And
peat the sound - ing joy, Re - peat, re -
won - ders of His love, And won - ders,
D
Em
D
A7
D
heav'n and na - ture sing.
peat the sound - ing joy.
won - ders of His love.

THE LITTLE DRUMMER BOY

Words and Music by
KATHERINE DAVIS,
HENRY ONORATI
and HARRY SIMEONE

© 1958 (Renewed 1986) EMI MILLS MUSIC, INC. and INTERNATIONAL KORWIN CORP.
Worldwide Print Rights on behalf of EMI MILLS MUSIC, INC. Administered by WARNER BROS. PUBLICATIONS U.S. INC.
All Rights Reserved

F
B♭
rum pum pum pum, To lay be - fore the King, pa -
rum pum pum pum, That's fit to give our King, pa -
F7
B♭
F
C
rum pum pum pum, rum pum pum pum, rum pum pum pum,
rum pum pum pum, rum pum pum pum, rum pum pum pum,
F
So to hon - or Him, pa - rum pum pum pum,
Shall I play for you, pa - rum pum pum pum,
1. C7
F
when we come.
f

2.
C7
F
on my drum?
l.h.
f
F
Mar - y nod - ded, pa - rum pum pum pum,
The Ox and Lamb kept time, pa - rum pum pum pum.
C
I played my drum for Him, pa - rum pum pum pum,

F
Bb
F7
Bb
F
I played my best for Him, pa - rum pum pum pum, rum pum pum pum,
C
rum pum pum pum.
r.h.
l.h.
F
Then He smiled at me pa - rum pum pum pum,
C7
F
me and my drum.
f

LITTLE SAINT NICK

Words and Music by
BRIAN WILSON

© 1963 (Renewed 1991) IRVING MUSIC, INC. (BMI)
This Arrangement © 1979 IRVING MUSIC, INC. (BMI)
All Rights Reserved

Am7
D7
Am7
D7
G
1. Way up north where the air gets cold, There's a tale about Christ-mas that you've
2. lit-tle bob-sled we call it old Saint Nick, But she'll walk the to-bog-gan with a
G#o
Am7
D7
Am7
D7
all been told. And a real fa-mous cat all dressed up in red, And he
four-speed stick; She's can-dy-ap-ple red with a ski for a wheel. And when
G
C
spends his whole year work-ing out in his sled
San-ta gives the gas, man just watch her peel.
It's the Lit-tle Saint Nick (Lit-tle
(group)
Am7
1.
D7
Saint Nick) It's the Lit-tle Saint Nick (Lit-tle Saint Nick) 2. Just a
(solo)
(group)
(solo)

2.
D7
C
F
Saint Nick.)
(group)
Run, run, rein - deer
Run, run, rein - deer
sim
C
A
Run, run, rein - deer
Run, run, rein - deer
Am7
D7
Am7
D7
(solo)
He's
haul - in' through the snow at a
fright -'nin' speed, with a
Run, run, run, yeah
(solo)
G
G#o
Am7
D7
half doz - en deer, with
Ru - dy to lead.
He's
got to wear gog - gles cuz the

Am7
D7
G
snow real-ly flies, and he's cruis-in' ev-'ry pad with a lit-tle sur-prise; It's the
C
G
Lit-tle Saint Nick (Lit-tle Saint Nick) It's the Lit-tle Saint Nick (Lit-tle
G♯o
Am7
D7
Saint Nick) (group) Oo Mer-ry Christ-mas Saint
1. thru 7.
8.
G
G♯o
G
Nick
(Run, run, run, yeah etc.)
Nick.

A MERRY, MERRY CHRISTMAS TO YOU

(Joyeux Noel, Buon Natale, Feliz Navidad)

By JOHNNY MARKS

© 1958 (Renewed 1986) ST. NICHOLAS MUSIC, INC.
All Rights Reserved Used by Permission

C♯dim
B♭
G7
To Coda
C7
F7
B♭
ring-ing with ev-'ry-one sing-ing A Mer - ry Christ-mas to you!
Interlude
Dm
Gm6
Dm
*Joy - eux No - el, Buon - ne Na - tal - e,
(Jwah - yuh No - el, Bwon - ne Na - tahl - e,
mp
Gm6
A+
Dm
A7
Fe - liz - e Nav - i - dad. In ev - 'ry land there's a
Fe - leath - e Nav - ee - dahd.)
Dm
C7
F7
D. S. al Coda
(**)
way of say-ing what we want to say. Oh!
f
Coda
C7
F7
C7
F7
C7
F7
Cm7
F7
B♭
Mer - ry Christ-mas, A Mer - ry Christ-mas, A Mer - ry Christ-mas to you!
8va
rall.
f
sfz
*Use any language desired. (**) Can repeat full chorus then 4 bar vamp shouting languages, then Coda

THE MOST WONDERFUL DAY OF THE YEAR

Words and Music by
JOHNNY MARKS

© 1964 (Renewed 1992) ST. NICHOLAS MUSIC, INC.
This Arrangement © 1970 ST. NICHOLAS MUSIC, INC.
All Rights Reserved Used by Permission

C
C6
C
D7
on the floor. There's no room for
more And it's all be - cause of San - ta Claus! A
G9
C♯dim
Dm7
G7
scoot - er for Jim - my, a dol - ly for Sue. The kind that will
A7
Dm
e - ven say "How do you do!" When Christ - mas Day is
A7+5
D♯dim
here The most won - der - ful day of the year.

THE NIGHT BEFORE CHRISTMAS SONG

Lyric adapted by
JOHNNY MARKS
From Clement Moore's Poem

Music by
JOHNNY MARKS

© 1952 (Renewed 1980) ST. NICHOLAS MUSIC, INC.
This Arrangement © 1970 ST. NICHOLAS MUSIC, INC.
All Rights Reserved Used by Permission

F C Dm
what to my won - der - ing eyes should ap - pear, A min - ia - ture
spoke not a word but went straight to his work And filled all the
G9 C C7 F F♯dim
sleigh and eight ti - ny rein - deer. A lit - tle old driv - er so
stock - ings; then turned with a jerk. And lay - ing his fin - ger a -
C A7 D7 Dm7
live - ly and quick, I knew in a mo - ment it must be Saint
side of his nose, then giv - ing a nod up the chim - ney he
G7 C Em F C
Nick. And more rap - id than ea - gles his rein - deer all came, As he
rose; But I heard him ex - claim as he drove out of sight, "Mer - ry
Dm C 1. G7 C 2. G7 C
shout - ed, "On Dash - er" and each rein - deer's name. And so
Christ - mas to all and to all a Good Night!"

THE WONDERFUL WORLD OF CHRISTMAS

Words by
CHARLES TOBIAS

Music by
AL FRISCH

TRO © 1968 and 1969 HAMPSHIRE HOUSE PUBLISHING CORP.
All Rights Reserved Used by Permission

G Gmaj7 Am7 D7 Am7 D7 Gmaj7 G7
smile and good cheer of each neigh-bor and chil-dren with cheeks all a-glow So
C B♭dim G (B Bass) Am7 D7 G
A little faster
Gmaj7 Am (G Bass)
warm is the Christ-mas-y feel-ing with the tree-tops all wrapped up in snow. Lis-ten to those
mf
Gmaj7 Am (G Bass) Gmaj7 Am (G Bass) Gmaj7 Am (G Bass) Gmaj7 Am (G Bass) Gmaj7 Am (G Bass)
won-d'rous bells and you'll hear them say, "O-pen up your hearts to all
1st tempo
Gmaj7 Am (G Bass) D7 G D7 G Gmaj7 Am7 D7 Am7 D7
on this hol-i-day." The won-der-ful world of Christ-mas is a joy from the mo-ment it
rall.
mp
Gmaj7 G7 C B♭dim G (B Bass) Am7 D7 Gsus4 G (D Bass) G
starts. The won-der-ful world of Christ-mas should re-main ev-'ry day in our hearts.
rall.

O CHRISTMAS TREE
(O Tannenbaum)

OLD GERMAN CAROL

© 1993 (Assigned) WARNER BROS. PUBLICATIONS INC.
All Rights Reserved including Public Performance for Profit

WHAT I LIKE THE MOST ABOUT CHRISTMAS

Words and Music by
JAMES DUNN

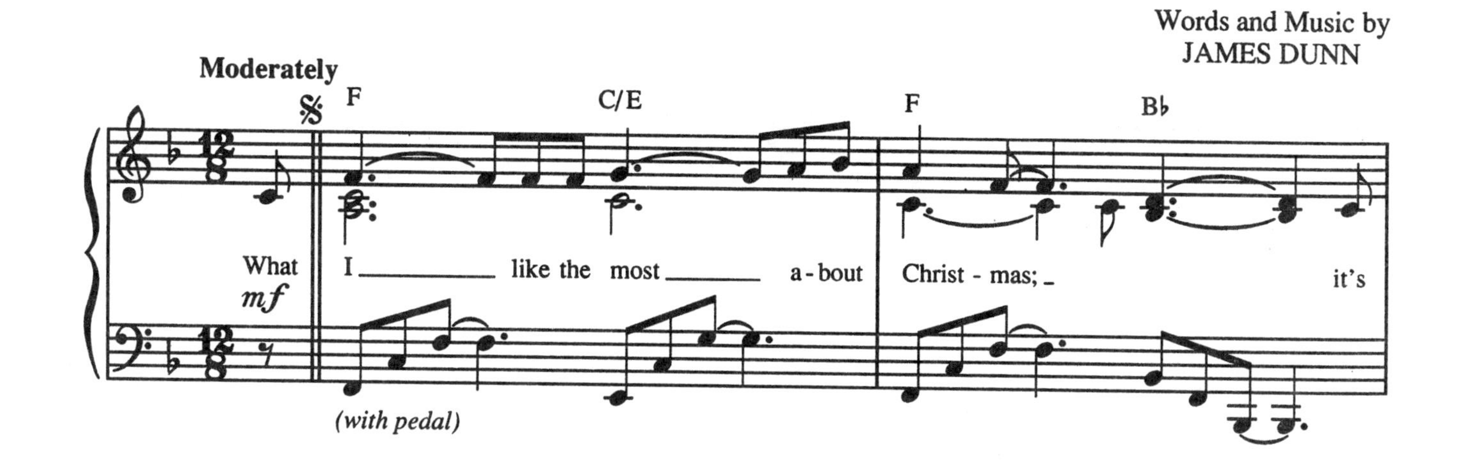

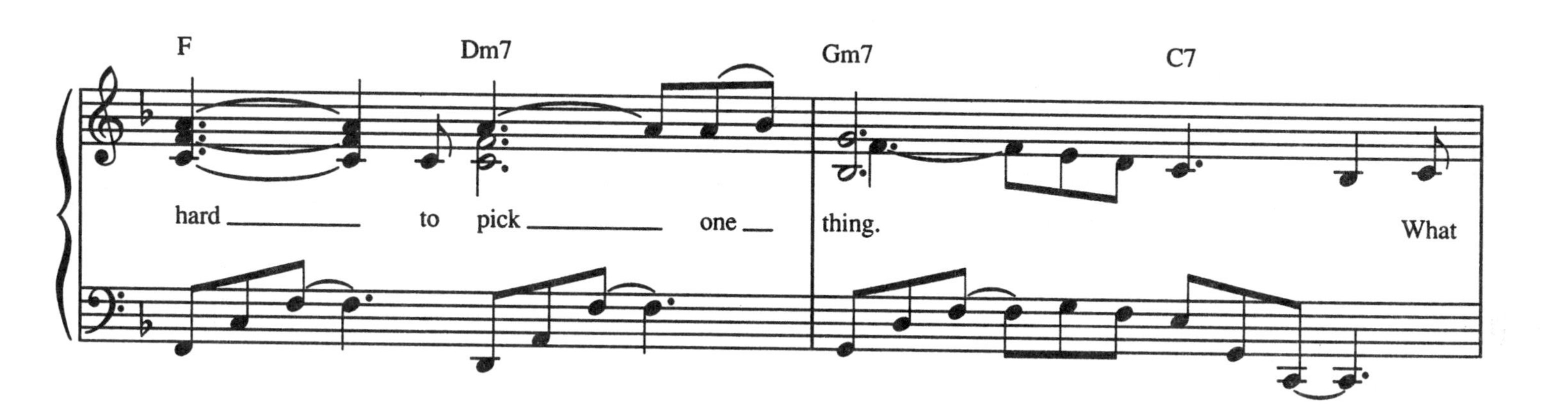

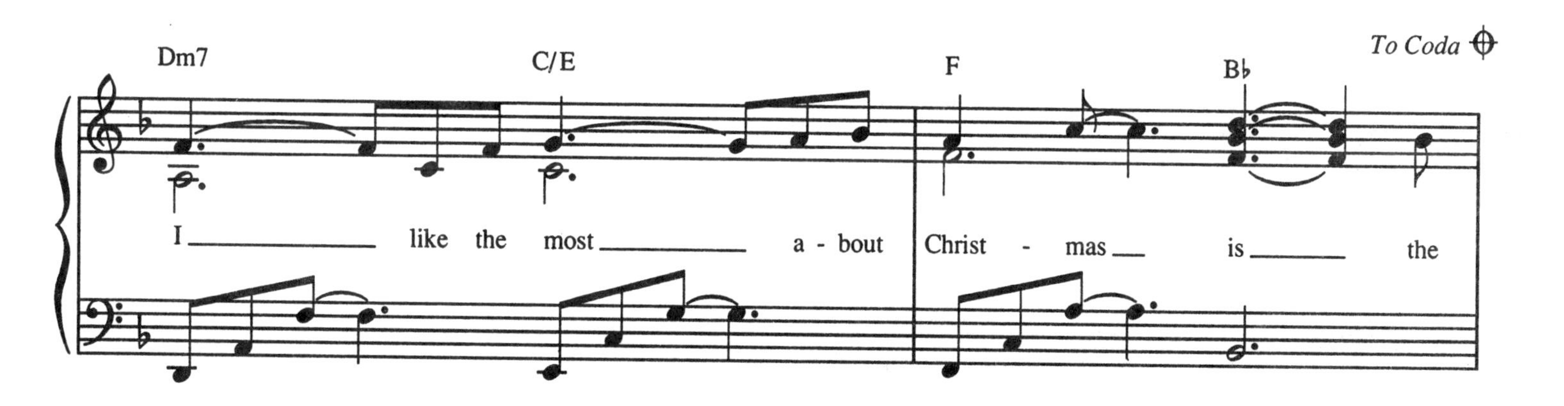

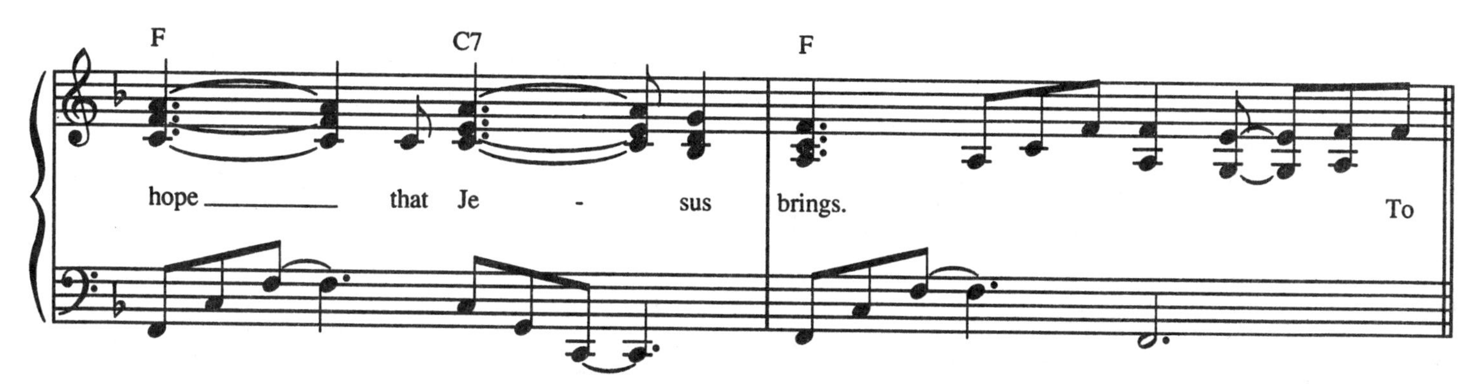

Copyright © 1992 by LAWLEY PUBLISHING
Administered by C.M.I.
International Copyright Secured Made in U.S.A. All Rights Reserved

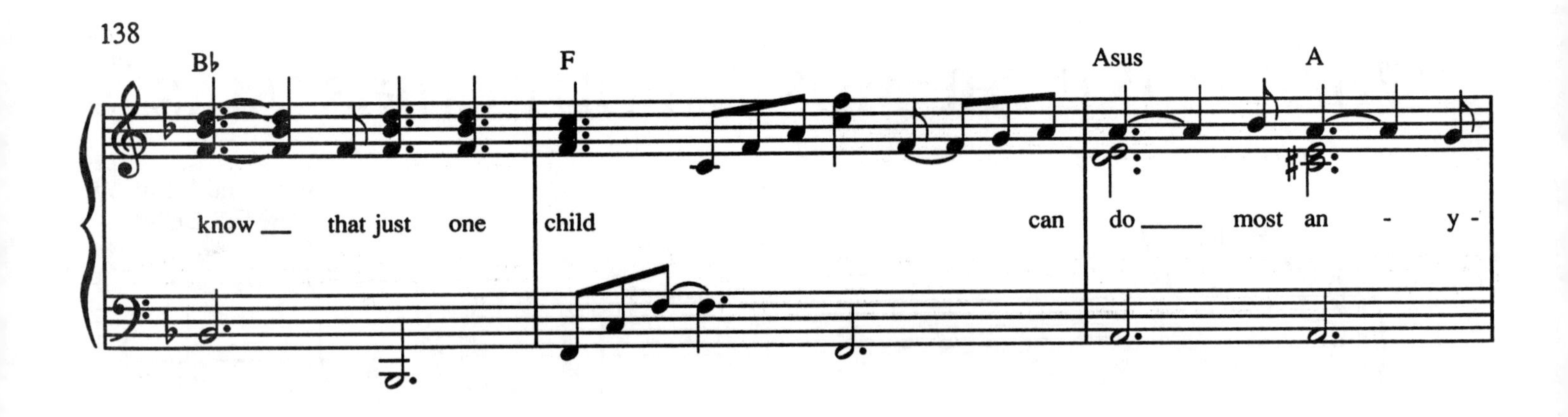
B♭
F
Asus
A
know — that just one child can do — most an - y -

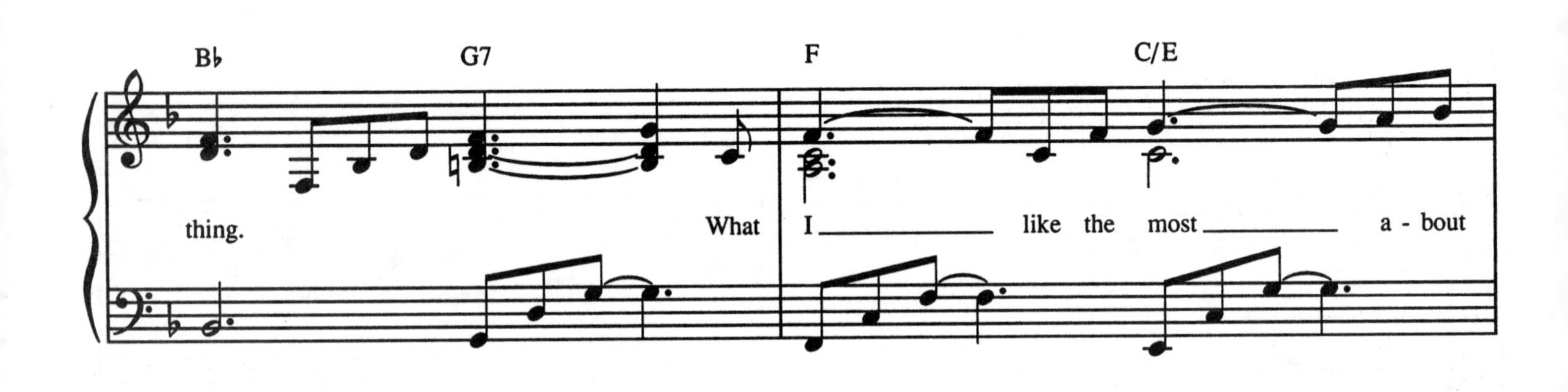
B♭
G7
F
C/E
thing. What I — like the most — a - bout

F
B♭
F
C7
F
Christ - mas — is — the hope — that Je - sus brings.

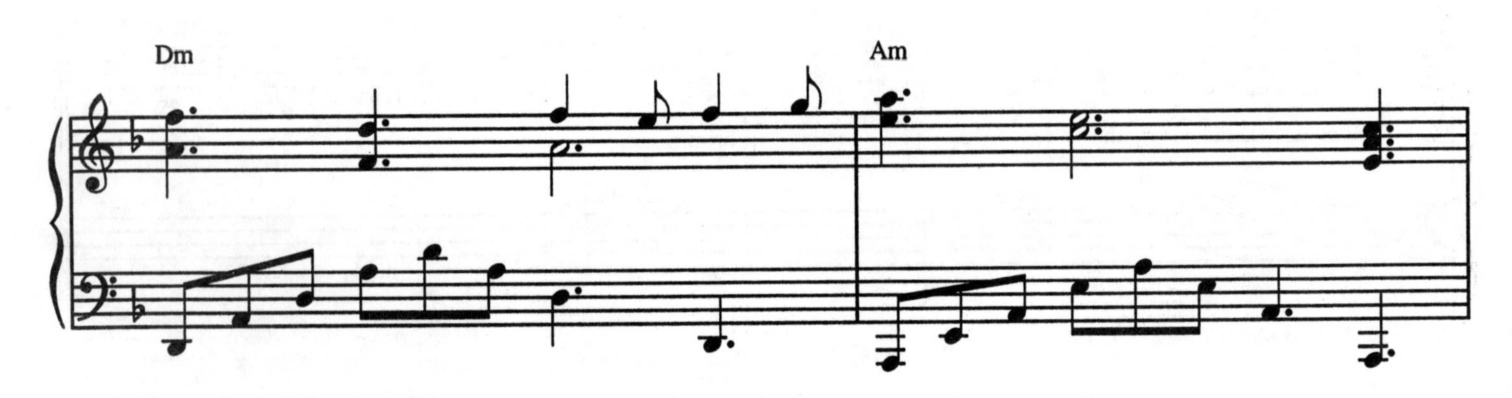
Dm
Am

B♭
4
F
Dm
Am
Gm7
C6
D.S. 𝄋 al Coda
B♭/C
C
What
Coda
F
C7
hope that Je - sus, the
F
B♭
hope that Je - sus, the
F
C7
hope that Je - sus
F
brings.

O COME, ALL YE FAITHFUL

(Adeste Fideles)

REV. F. OAKELEY

J. READING

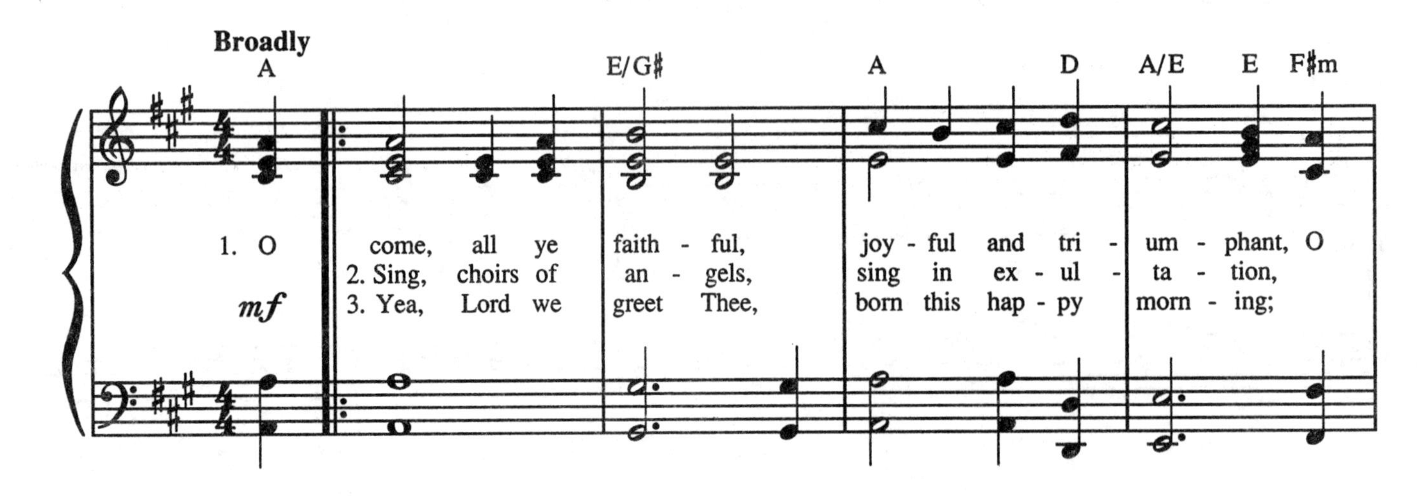

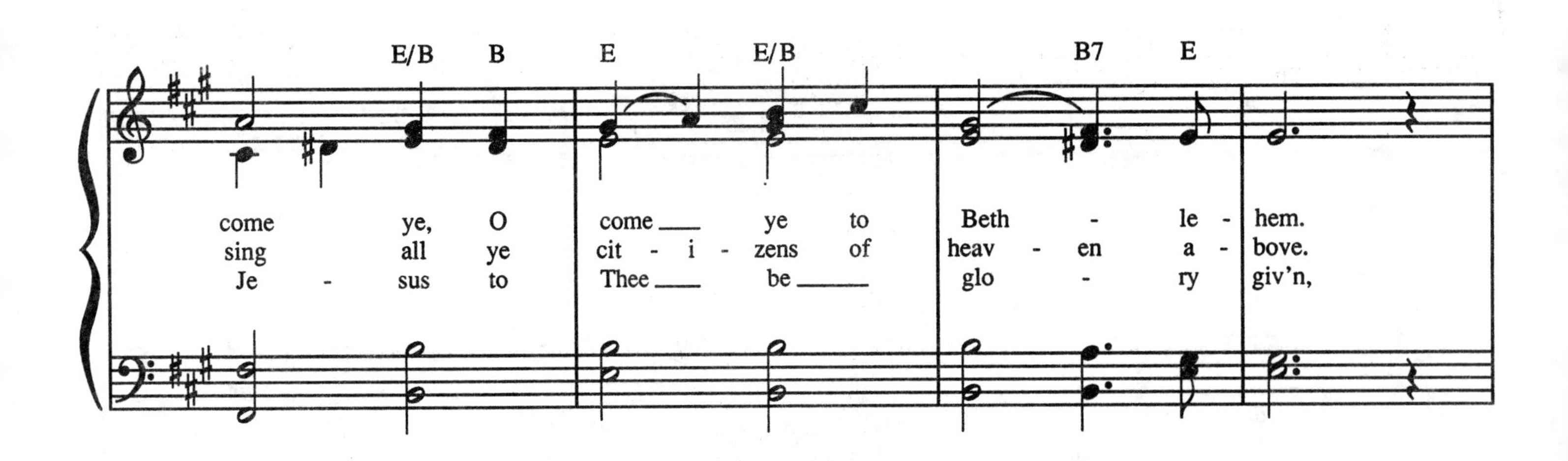

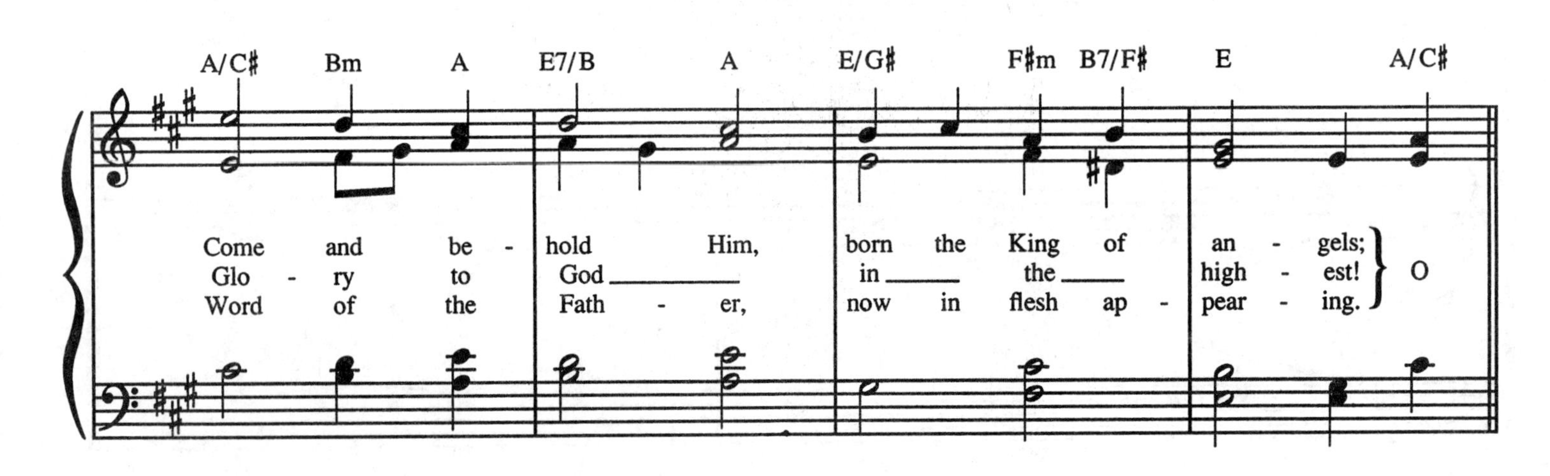

© 1991 (Assigned) WARNER BROS. PUBLICATIONS INC.
All Rights Reserved including Public Performance for Profit

Refrain:
A E/G♯ A E/B A E/G♯ A
come, let us a - dore Him, O come, let us a - dore Him, O

1.2.
3.
E7/B A E/G♯ B7/F♯ E A/C♯ D A/E E A A
come, let us a - dore Him, Christ the Lord. 2. O Lord.

O COME, O COME EMMANUEL

English Lyric by
JOHN M. NEALE
Traditional
Music adapted by
THOMAS HELMORE
Moderately
Em Bm Am Bm Em D
1. O come, o come, Em - man - u - el, and
2. O come, thou rod of Jes - se, free Thine
mf
G C Am Em Bm Em Am
ran - som cap - tive Is - ra - el, that
own from Sat - an's ty - ran - ny; from
C♯dim A A7 D Em
mourns in lone - ly ex - ile here, un -
depths of hell thy peo - ple save, and
O Come, O Come Emmanuel - 2 - 1
© 1978 ALMO MUSIC CORP. (ASCAP)
International Copyright Secured Made in U.S.A. All Rights Reserved

D
G
Am
Bm
G
Chorus:
til the Son of God ap - pear.
give them vict - 'ry o'er the grave. Re -
f
D
Em
Bm
G
Am
Bm
joice! Re - joice! Em - man - u -
Em
D7
G
C
Am
Em
Bm
Em
el shall come to thee, o Is - ra - el.

3. O come, Thou Day-Spring, come and cheer
Our spirits by Thine advent here;
Disperse the gloomy clouds of night,
And Death's dark shadows put to flight.
Chorus

4. O come, Thou Key of David, come,
And open wide our heav'nly home;
Make safe the way that leads on high,
And close the path to misery.
Chorus

5. O come, O come, Thou Lord of might,
Who to Thy tribes, on Sinai's height,
In ancient times did'st give the law,
In cloud, and majesty and awe.
Chorus

O HOLY NIGHT
(Cantique de Noel)

By ADOLPH ADAM

Moderate
C
Dm
C
G7
C
C
F
C
O ho - ly night! The stars are bright - ly shin - ing. It is the
G7
C
F
night of our dear Sav - iour's birth. Long lay the world in sin and er - ror
C
Em
B7
Em
G7
pin - ing, till He ap - pear'd and the soul felt its worth, A thrill of hope the

© 1978 (Assigned) WARNER BROS. PUBLICATIONS INC.
All Rights Reserved including Public Performance for Profit

C
G7
C
wear - y world re - joi - ces for yon - der breaks a new and glor - ious morn.
Am
Em
Dm
Am
Fall on your knees! Oh, hear the an - gel voi - ces! Oh,
C
G7
C
F
C
G7
C
night di - vine! O night when Christ was born, O
G7
C
Dm
C
G7
C
night di - vine, O night, O night di - vine.

O LITTLE TOWN OF BETHLEHEM

By L.H. REDNER

© 1978 (Assigned) WB MUSIC CORP. (ASCAP)
All Rights Administered by WARNER BROS. PUBLICATIONS U.S. INC.
All Rights Reserved including Public Performance for Profit

F
Dm
A
by; yet in thy dark streets shin - eth the
Dm
Bb
A
F
ev - er - last - ing light. The hopes and fears of
Bb
F
C7
F
all the years are met in thee to - night.

(There's Nothing Like)

AN OLD FASHIONED CHRISTMAS

Words and Music by
JOHNNY MARKS

Copyright © 1952, 1958 by ST. NICHOLAS MUSIC, INC.
This Arrangement Copyright © 1978 by ST. NICHOLAS MUSIC, INC. Used by Permission
International Copyright Secured Made in U.S.A. All Rights Reserved

C
C7
F
G#dim
floor. There's noth - ing like the old fav - 'rite
F
F7
Bb
E
A7
car - ols when neigh - bors come to call.
Ab
A7
D7
G7
So the best I can wish you,
Gm
Bbm
C7
F
is an old fash-ioned Christ-mas, that's all.
rit.
rit.

STAR OF THE EAST

Words by
GEORGE COOPER

Music by
AMANDA KENNEDY

Moderate
C7
F
C7
F
Bb
F
Star of the east, O Beth - le - hem's star,
Bb
C7
guid - ing us on to hea - ven a - far!
F
Bb
F
Sor - row and grief are lulled by thy light, thou

© 1978 (Assigned) WARNER BROS. PUBLICATIONS INC.
All Rights Reserved including Public Performance for Profit

C
F
C7
F
hope of each mor - tal, in death's lone - ly night!
Bb
F
Fear - less and tran - quil we look up to thee!
Help us to fol - low where thou still dost guide!
1. C7
F
Know - ing thou beams thru e - ter - ni - ty!
2. C7
Pil - grims of earth so wide.

ONCE IN ROYAL DAVID'S CITY

MRS. C.F. ALEXANDER

H.J. GAUNTLETT

2. He came down to earth from heaven,
Who is God and Lord of all,
And His shelter was a stable,
And His cradle was a stall.
With the poor and mean and lowly,
Lived on earth our Savior holy.

3. And our eyes at last shall see Him,
Through His own redeeming love,
For that Child so dear and gentle
Is our Lord in heaven above.
And He leads His children on
To the place where He is gone.

© 1969 (Assigned) WB MUSIC CORP. (ASCAP)
All Rights Administered by WARNER BROS. PUBLICATIONS U.S. INC.
All Rights Reserved including Public Performance for Profit

OUT OF THE EAST

Words and Music by
HARRY NOBLE

Moderato
Eb
Ebmaj7
Eb7
Ab
4 fr.
Eb
Bb9
p
Eb6(addF)
Eb6
Eb6(addF)
Eb6
Eb6
Eb6
l.h.
1. Out of the East there came
2. In - to the West they went
3. Low in a man - ger they
Fm7
Fm7
Abm6
Abm6
Eb6
Eb6
rid - ing, rid - ing, Three of the wis - est of men,
rid - ing, rid - ing, Fol - low-ing af - ter the star,
found Him, found Him, Bathed in the light of yon star,

© 1941 (Renewed 1968) THE BOSTON MUSIC COMPANY
Renewal © Assigned 1969 to LARRY SPIER, INC.
This Edition © 1974 LARRY SPIER, INC.
All Rights Reserved

Eb6 Eb6 Fm7 Fm7 Abm6 Abm6
Dust was their en - e - my blind - ing, blind - ing, E - ven the wis - est of
O - ver a qui - et town shin - ing, shin - ing, Light - ing their way from a -
Gold did they bring Him and frank - in - cense And myrhh from a land that was
simile
Eb6 Eb6 G7 G7 Cm Cm
mf
them. Wan - der - ing shep - herds heard tell their sto - ry,
far. Un - der its glo - ry sat moth - er Ma - ry,
far. Shep - herds crept in sing - ing prais - es, prais - es,
mf
F9 Cm7 F7 Bb7 Bb+ Gm Ab 4 fr. Bb7
dim. rit.
Told in the flick - er - ing fire - light, ten - der light, Ev - er bright Christ - mas night.
Ten - der - ly sing - ing a lull - a - bye, hush - a - bye, Don't you cry, lull - a - bye.
An - gels kept watch to be near to Him, dear to Him, One with Him, prais - ing Him.
dim. rit.

Eb6 Eb6 Fm7 Fm7 Abm6 Abm6 Eb6 Eb6
a tempo
p
Far to the West was there shin-ing shin-ing, Blaz-ing a star in the dawn;
In-to the sta-ble came rid-ing, rid-ing, Three of the wis-est of men;
In-to the East then went rid-ing, rid-ing, Three of the wis-est of men;
p a tempo
Ped.
Eb6 Eb6 Fm7 Fm7 Abm6 Abm6
1.2.
Eb Ebmaj7 Eb7
rit.
a tempo
Rev-er-ent wise men be-held it, say-ing, This night a Sav-ior is born.
Gifts did they bring for that babe in man-ger, Gifts for the Sav-ior of men.
Found was the babe in a low-ly man-ger, Crowned was the Sav-ior of
rit.
p a tempo
simile
Ab Eb Bb9 Eb6(addF) Eb6 Eb6(addF) Eb6
4 fr.
3.
Eb6 Eb6 Eb6 Eb6
men.
l.h.
Ped.

ONCE UPON A CHRISTMAS

Words and Music by
DOLLY PARTON

Slowly, with expression ♩= 66
f mf
poco rit.
Am
Am
C
Spoken: 1. Once upon a Christmas
Sung: 2. Once up-on_ a Christ-mas in a
a tempo
dim.
mp-mf
Am
G
far away in Bethlehem,
man - ger far a - way a
Mary, being great with child,
King was born; His pal - ace was a

Copyright ©1984 VELVET APPLE MUSIC (BMI)
International Copyright Secured Made In U.S.A. All Rights Reserved

D
Am
C
had no place to lie down. So Joseph found a stable in
man - ger filled with hay. His roy - al robe _ was swad - dling cloth; a
Am
G
which Mary had her child. Once upon a Christmas was
ha - lo was His crown, once up-on _ a Christ-mas a -
D
1. Am
2.3. Am
the birth of Jesus Christ.
way in Beth - le - hem. And

Chorus:
G
D
G
all the world re-joiced be-cause the King was born at last. A
f
D
G
sav - iour had been prom - ised, now it had come to pass. And the
Em
G
Em
joy - ful news that He was born spread quick - ly far and wide

D
Em
1.
E
D
D.S.
2.
E
D/F#
once up-on _ a Christ-mas, and the birth of Je - sus Christ. Christ.
dim.
cresc.
3.
E
D(add 9)
Am
C
Am
Christ. Once up-on _ a Christ - mas far a - way in Beth - le - hem.
mp
molto rit. e dim.
p

Verse 3:
Once upon a Christmas from the Far East wise men came
With gold and myrrh and frankincense to praise the newborn King.
And shepherds left their flocks and came to see and worship Him
Once upon a Christmas away in Bethlehem.

(To Chorus:)

From the Videocraft T.V. Musical Spectacular "RUDOLPH, THE RED-NOSED REINDEER"

SILVER AND GOLD

Words and Music by
JOHNNY MARKS

© 1964 ST. NICHOLAS MUSIC, INC.
This Arrangement © 1970 by ST. NICHOLAS MUSIC, INC.
All Rights Reserved Used by Permission

UP ON THE HOUSE-TOP

Words and Music by
BENJAMIN RUSSELL HANBY

© 1964 (Renewed 1992 & Assigned) WB MUSIC CORP. (ASCAP)
All Rights Administered by WARNER BROS. PUBLICATIONS U.S. INC.
All Rights Reserved including Public Performance for Profit

THE THREE KINGS

© 1958 WARNER BROS. INC. (Renewed)
All Rights Reserved

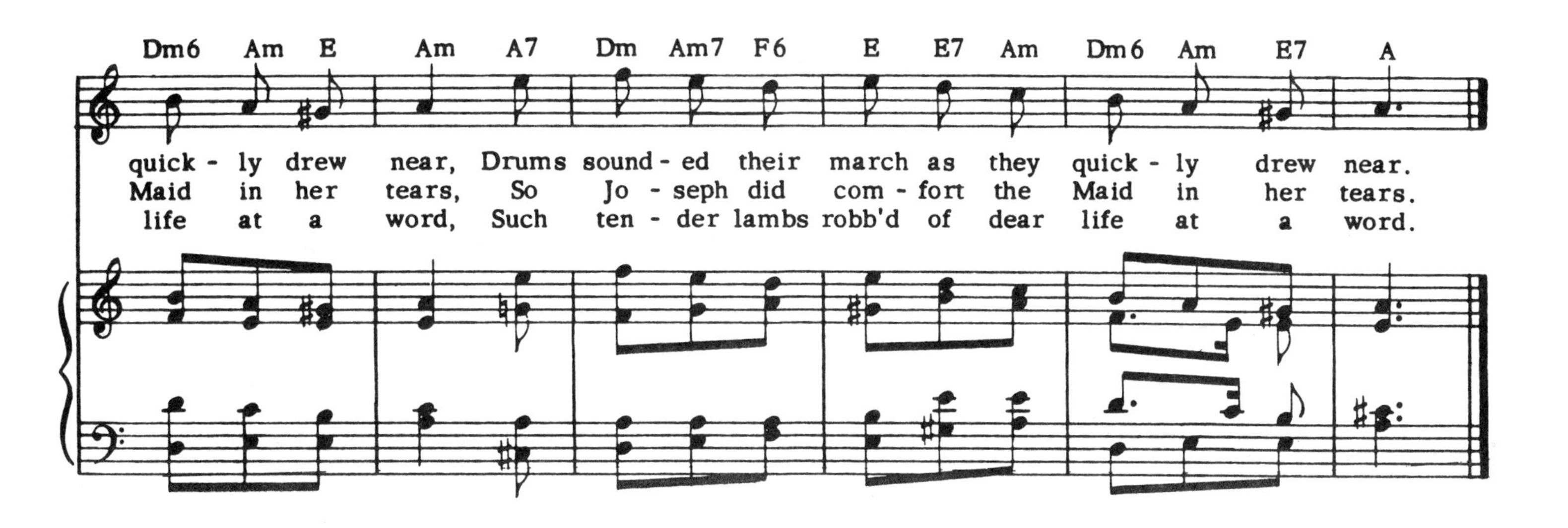
Dm6 Am E Am A7 Dm Am7 F6 E E7 Am Dm6 Am E7 A
quick - ly drew near, Drums sound - ed their march as they quick - ly drew near.
Maid in her tears, So Jo - seph did com - fort the Maid in her tears.
life at a word, Such ten - der lambs robb'd of dear life at a word.

THERE IS NO CHRISTMAS LIKE A HOME CHRISTMAS

Words by
CARL SIGMAN

Music by
MICKEY J. ADDY

© 1950 RONCOM MUSIC CO.
© Renewed 1977 MAJOR SONGS COMPANY and LIBRELLE MUSIC COMPANY
All Rights on behalf of LIBRELLE MUSIC COMPANY for the World outside the U.S. and Canada Administered by WB MUSIC CORP. (ASCAP)
All Rights Reserved

F F+ F6 F F+ F6 F G6 G7 C
Christ-mas bells, Christ-mas bells, ring - ing loud and strong,
mf
Am E+ Am7 D9 Dm7 C#dim7 Dm C#dim7 Dm7 G7
Tacet
Fol - low them, fol - low them, you've been a - way too long. There is
mp
C Gm7 C7 F Ab7
no Christ - mas like a home Christ - mas, for
C G7 Fmaj7 Em7 Dm7 G9 C Cmaj7 C7 F Fm C
that's the time of year all roads lead home.
f
dim.
rall.

UKRANIAN CAROL

Traditional

© 1982 (Assigned) WB MUSIC CORP. (ASCAP)
All Rights Administered by WARNER BROS. PUBLICATIONS U.S. INC.
All Rights Reserved including Public Performances for Profit

ff
mf
1.
dim. (without rit.)
p
pp
2.
dim.
(without rit.)
pp
mf
(slowly)

From the Videocraft T.V. Musical Spectacular "RUDOLPH, THE RED-NOSED REINDEER"

WE ARE SANTA'S ELVES

By JOHNNY MARKS

Gaily
Gm
F♯dim
Gm
F♯dim
Gm
C7
F
B♭
Am
C7
F
Ho! Ho! Ho! Ho! Ho! Ho! We are San - ta's elves!
C7
We are San - ta's elves, fil - ling San - ta's shelves
We work hard all day, but our work is play.
San - ta knows who's good; do the things you should!

© 1964 (Renewed 1992) ST. NICHOLAS MUSIC, INC.
This Arrangement @ 1978 ST. NICHOLAS MUSIC, INC.
All Rights Reserved Used by Permission

F
C7
F7
B♭
B♭m
F
C7
F
to CODA
with a toy for each girl and boy. Oh, we are San - ta's elves!
Dolls we try out, see if they cry out, we are San - ta's elves!
And we bet you, he won't for - get you, we are San - ta's elves!
B♭
Am
Gm
Dm
F♯dim
We've a spe - cial job each year, we don't like to brag.
C
C♯dim
Dm
G7
C7
D.S. al CODA
Christ-mas Eve we al-ways fill San - ta's bag!
CODA
Gm
F♯dim
Gm
F♯dim
Gm
C7
F
Ho! Ho! Ho! Ho! Ho! Ho! We are San - ta's elves! Ho! Ho!

A GREAT AND MIGHTY WONDER

GERMAN

© 1978 (Assigned) WB MUSIC CORP. (ASCAP)
All Rights Administered by WARNER BROS. PUBLICATIONS INC.
All Rights Reserved including Public Performance for Profit

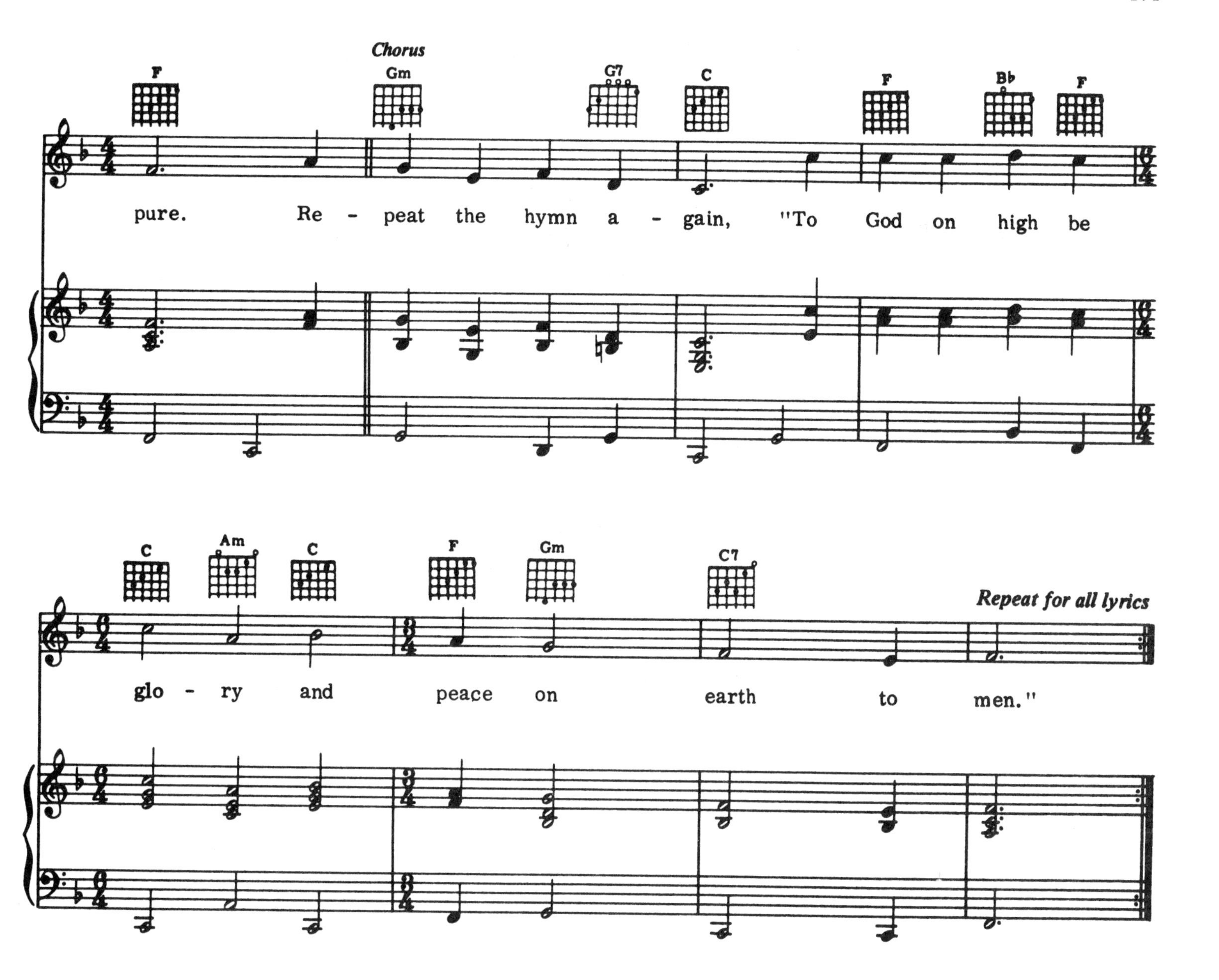
Chorus
F
Gm
G7
C
F
Bb
F
pure. Re - peat the hymn a - gain, "To God on high be
C
Am
C
F
Gm
C7
Repeat for all lyrics
glo - ry and peace on earth to men."

2. The Word becomes incarnate
   And yet remains on high!
   And cherubim sing anthems
   To shepherds from the sky.

3. While thus they sing your Monarch,
   Those bright angelic bands
   Rejoice, ye vales and mountains,
   Ye oceans, clap your hands.

4. Since all He comes to ransom,
   By all be He adorned,
   The infant born in Bethl'em,
   The Saviour and the Lord.

5. And idol forms shall perish,
   And error shall decay,
   And Christ shall wield His sceptre,
   Our Lord and God for aye.

WHEN SANTA CLAUS GETS YOUR LETTER

Words and Music by
JOHNNY MARKS

© 1950 (Renewed 1978) ST. NICHOLAS MUSIC, INC.
This Arrangement © 1970 ST. NICHOLAS MUSIC, INC.
All Rights Reserved Used by Permission

F B7 C Cdim C C7
stroke his beard, his eyes will glow and at your name he'll peer; It
F E♭dim D7 G7
takes a lit - tle time you know, to check back one whole year! When
C Cdim C G7 C G7
San - ta Claus gets your let - ter, I real - ly do be - lieve, You'll
Am Em Dm C A7 D7 G7
head his list, you won't be missed by San - ta on Christ - mas
1. C Dm7 G7
eve. When
2. C Am Dm7 G7 C
eve.

WHILE SHEPHERDS WATCHED THEIR FLOCKS BY NIGHT

Words by
REV. NAHUM TATE

Music by
GEORGE F. HANDEL

3. "To you, in David's town, this day
Is born of David's line,
The Saviour Who is Christ the Lord;
And this shall be the sign;
And this shall be the sign."

4. "The Heav'nly Babe you there shall find
To human view displayed,
All meanly wrapped in swathingbands,
And in a manger laid,
And in a manger laid."

5. "All glory be to God on high,
And to the earth be peace:
Goodwill hence forth from heav'n to men,
Begin and never cease:
Begin and never cease."

Copyright © 1978 ALMO MUSIC CORP. (ASCAP)
International Copyright Secured Made In U.S.A. All Rights Reserved

WINTER WONDERLAND

Words by
DICK SMITH

Music by
FELIX BERNARD

© 1934 WB MUSIC CORP. (Renewed)
All Rights Reserved

E7
Eb7
Eb
Bb7
Love knows no sea - son; love knows no clime;
ro-mance can blos - som an-y old time;
Cm
Here in the o - pen, we're
F7
walk - in' and hop - in' to - geth - er!
Refrain:
Sleigh - bells ring, are you lis - t'nin'? In the
Sleigh - bells ring, are you lis - t'nin'? In the
p-f

Bb7
lane, snow is glis - t'nin', a beau - ti - ful sight, we're
lane, snow is glis - t'nin', a beau - ti - ful sight, we're
F7
Bb7
Eb
hap - py to - night, walk - in' in a win - ter won - der - land! Gone a -
hap - py to - night, walk - in' in a win - ter won - der - land! Gone a -
Bb7
way is the blue - bird, here to stay is a
way is the blue - bird, here to stay is a
new bird; He sings a love song, as we go a - long,
new bird; He's sing - ing a song, as we go a - long,

F7
Bb7
Eb
walk - in' in a win - ter won - der - land!
walk - in' in a win - ter won - der - land!
G
D7
G
In the mead - ow we can build a snow - man,
In the mead - ow we can build a snow - man,
D7
G
Then pre - tend that he is Par - son Brown;
And pre - tend that he's a cir - cus clown;
Bb
F7
Bb
He'll say, "Are you mar - ried?" We'll say, "No, man! But
We'll have lots of fun with Mis - ter Snow - man, Un -

C7
F7
Eb7
you can do the job when you're in town!" Lat - er
til the oth - er kid - dies knock 'im down! When it
Eb
Bb7
on, we'll con - spire, as we dream by the
snows, ain't it thrill - in', Tho' your nose gets a
fire, to face un - a - fraid, the plans that we made,
chill - in'? We'll frol - ic and play the Es - ki - mo way,
F7
Bb7
Eb
Bb7
Eb
1.
2.
walk - in' in a win - ter won - der - land! Sleigh - bells
walk - in' in a win - ter won - der - land!

THE TWELVE DAYS OF CHRISTMAS

Traditional

© 1978 (Assigned) WARNER BROS. PUBLICATIONS INC.
All Rights Reserved including Public Performance for Profit

G
C
G
D7
G
to Verse 4
two tur - tle doves, and a par - tridge_ in a pear tree. On the
4.
D7
four call - ing birds, three French_ hens, two tur - tle doves, and a
G
C
G
D7
G
to Verse 5
5. G
A7
D
D7
par - tridge_ in a pear tree. On the five gold - en rings,

G
C
A7
D
four___ call - ing birds, three French hens, two___ tur - tle doves, and a
G
C
G
D7
G
End here
(after all Verses)
par - tridge___ in a pear tree.
6. On the
7. On the
8. On the
9. On the
10. On the
11. On the
12.. On the
D7
G
D7
sixth day of
seventh day of
eighth day of
ninth day of
tenth day of
eleventh day of
twelvth day of
Christ - mas my true love sent to me
6. six geese a - lay - ing. (go to ending 5)
7. seven swans a - swim - ming. (to 6)
8. eight maids a - milk - ing. (to 7)
9. nine la - dies danc - ing. (to 8)
10. ten lords a - leap - ing. (to 9)
11. eleven pi - pers pip - ing. (to 10)
12. twelve drum - mers drum-ming. (to 11)

RUDOLPH, THE RED-NOSED REINDEER

Words and Music by
JOHNNY MARKS

© 1949 (Renewed 1977) ST. NICHOLAS MUSIC, INC.
All Rights Reserved Used by Permission

G7
G7(♯5)
C
nose, and if you ev - er saw it, you would e - ven say it glows.
E♭dim7
G7
All of the oth - er rein - deer used to laugh and call him names.
C
C7
They nev - er let poor Ru - dolph join in an - y rein - deer games.
F
C
C7
Dm
G7
C
C♯dim7
Then one fog - gy Christ - mas Eve, San - ta came to say:

G
Gmaj7
G♯dim7
Am
Am7
D7
G7
"Ru - dolph, with your nose so bright, won't you guide my sleigh to - night;" _
C
E♭dim7
G7
Then how the rein - deer loved him as they shout-ed out with glee:
1.
C
"Ru-dolph, the red - nosed rein - deer, you'll go down in his - to - ry."
Gdim7
G7
2.
C
Gdim7
G7
C
ry." ___
3

ANGELS WE HAVE HEARD ON HIGH

Traditional

Joyously

G E7 Am D/F♯ Em C A/C♯ Dsus D

f

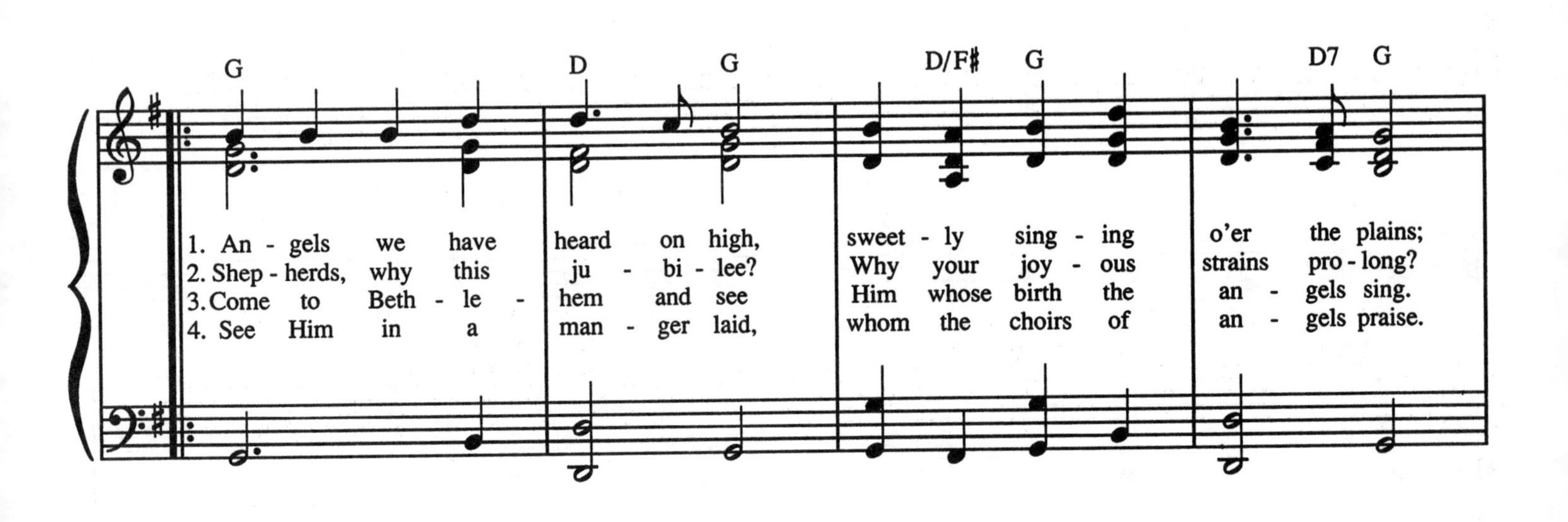
G D G D/F♯ G D7 G
1. An - gels we have heard on high, sweet - ly sing - ing o'er the plains;
2. Shep - herds, why this ju - bi - lee? Why your joy - ous strains pro - long?
3. Come to Beth - le - hem and see Him whose birth the an - gels sing.
4. See Him in a man - ger laid, whom the choirs of an - gels praise.

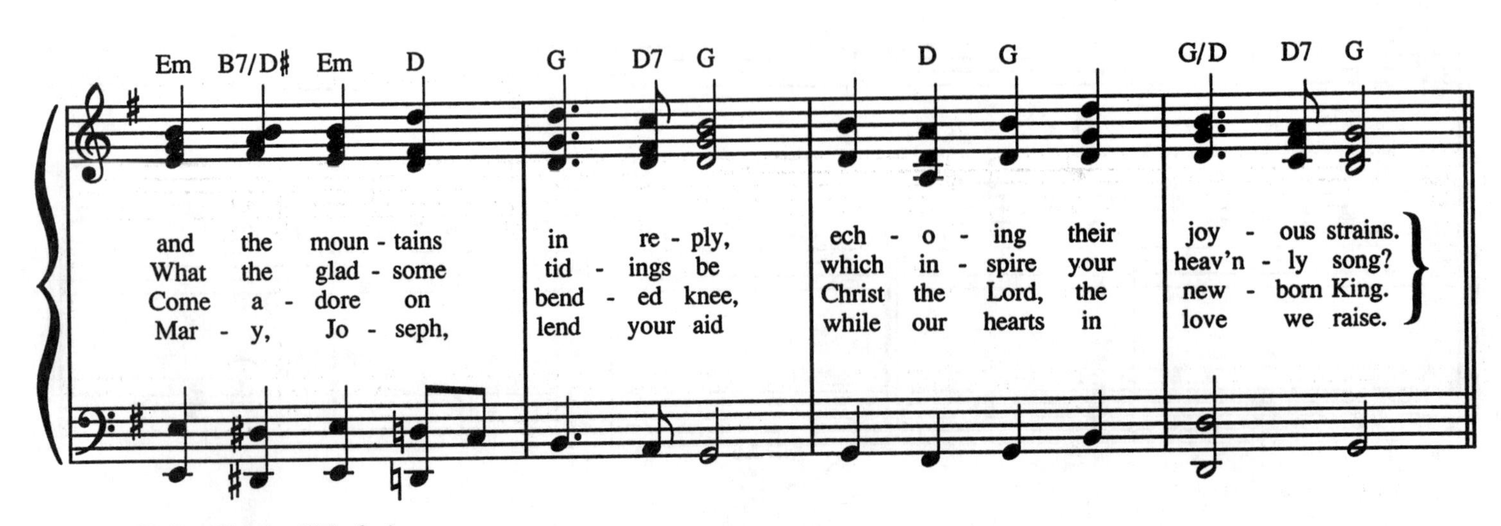
Em B7/D♯ Em D G D7 G D G G/D D7 G
and the moun - tains in re - ply, ech - o - ing their joy - ous strains.
What the glad - some tid - ings be which in - spire your heav'n - ly song?
Come a - dore on bend - ed knee, Christ the Lord, the new - born King.
Mar - y, Jo - seph, lend your aid while our hearts in love we raise.

© 1991 (Assigned) WARNER BROS. PUBLICATIONS INC.
All Rights Reserved including Public Performance for Profit

G
E7
Am
D7/F♯
Em
C
Dsus
D
Glo - - - ri - a
f
G
D
G
Am/C
G/D
D
G
E7
in ex - cel - sis De - o, Glo -
Am
D7
Em
C
A7/C♯
Dsus
D
- - ri - a
G
D
G
Am/C
G/D
D7
1.2.3.
G
4.
G
in ex - cel - sis De - o. o.

SANTA CLAUS IS COMIN' TO TOWN

Words by
HAVEN GILLESPIE

Music by
J. FRED COOTS

© 1934 (Renewed 1962) EMI FEIST CATALOG INC.
Rights for the Extended Renewal Term in the United States Controlled by HAVEN GILLESPIE MUSIC and EMI FEIST CATALOG INC.
All Rights outside the United States Controlled by EMI FEIST CATALOG INC. (Publishing) and WARNER BROS. PUBLICATIONS U.S. INC. (Print)
All Rights Reserved

C7 F C7
He sees you when you're sleep-in', He knows when you're a -
F D7 G D7
wake, He knows if you've been bad or good, So be good for good - ness
G G+ C C7 F Fm C C7
sake. Oh! You bet - ter watch out, you bet - ter not cry, Bet-ter not pout I'm
F Fm C Am Dm G7 C
tell - ing you why: San - ta Claus is com - in' to town.

WE WISH YOU A MERRY CHRISTMAS

Traditional English Carol

© 1977 (Assigned) WARNER BROS. PUBLICATIONS INC.
All Rights Reserved including Public Performance for Profit

A7
D
G
B7
Em
Am7
like fig-gy fig-gy pud-ding, We like fig-gy fig-gy pud-ding and a
C6
D7
G
C
A
cup of good cheer. 4. We won't go un-til we've got some, we won't go un-til we've
D
G
B7
Em
Am7
A7
D7
got some, We won't go un-til we've got some, Kind-ly bring some out
G
B7
C
Am7
D
D7
G
here. We wish you a Mer-ry Christ-mas and a hap-py New Year.
f

SILENT NIGHT

Words and Music by
JOSEPH MOHR and
FRANZ GRUBER

Slow
C
G7
F
mp
Si - lent Night, Ho - ly Night, All is calm,
all is bright, round yon vir - gin Moth - er and child.
Ho - ly in - fant so ten - der and mild. Sleep in heav - en - ly

© 1977 (Assigned) WB MUSIC CORP. (ASCAP)
All Rights Administered by WARNER BROS. PUBLICATIONS U.S. INC.
All Rights Reserved including Public Performance for Profit

C
G7
C
peace, sleep in heav - en - ly peace! Si - lent Night,
G7
C
Ho - ly Night, Shep - herds quake at the sight;
F
C
F
Glor - ies stream from heav - en a - far, Heav - en - ly hosts sing
C
G7
C
Al - le - lu - ia, Christ the sav - ior, is born!

G7
C
Christ, the savior is born! Si - lent Night, Ho - ly Night,
G7
C
F
Son of God, love's pure light, Ra - diant beams from
C
F
C
Thy ho - ly face, with the dawn of re - deem - ing grace,
G7
C
G7
C
Je - sus Lord at Thy birth. Je - sus Lord at Thy birth.

WE THREE KINGS OF ORIENT ARE

JOHN H. HOPKINS

© 1964 (Assigned) WB MUSIC CORP. (ASCAP)
All Rights Administered by WARNER BROS. PUBLICATIONS U.S. INC.
All Rights Reserved including Public Performance for Profit

Super Sellers

Personality Collections

GARTH BROOKS/
BEYOND THE SEASON
____ (P0957SMX) Piano/Vocal/Chords

Album-matching folio featuring old Christmas favorites along with a few originals. The 10 titles include: The Friendly Beasts • The Gift • God Rest Ye Merry, Gentlemen • The Old Man's Back in Town • Santa Looked a Lot Like Daddy • Silent Night • What Child Is This?

CARPENTERS/
CHRISTMAS PORTRAIT
____ (P0673SMX)

Seventeen songs from the Carpenter's Christmas album. An overture medley • Ave Maria • Christmas Song • Christmas Waltz • First Snowfall • It's Christmas Time • O Come, O Come Immanuel • Sleigh Ride and more popular and traditional favorites.

VINCE GUARALDI TRIO/
A CHARLIE BROWN CHRISTMAS
____ (P0924SMX) Piano Solo/ Vocal/Chords
____ (P0924P2X) Easy Piano

Music from the highly acclaimed PEANUTS® Christmas special in a sheet music folio. Titles are: Christmas Is Coming • The Christmas Song • Greensleeves • Christmas Time Is Here • Für Elise • Hark, The Herald Angels Sing • My Little Drum • O Tannenbaum • Skating • What Child Is This and Linus and Lucy.

HENRY MANCINI/
A MERRY MANCINI CHRISTMAS
____ (P0734P9X)

Henry Mancini's beautiful orchestrations adapted for piano/vocal by Tom Roed. Traditional and popular tunes combined with some superb medleys. Titles include: Winter Wonderland and Silver Bells Medley • The Christmas Song • Med-ley of Silent Night, O Holy Night • O Little Town of Bethlehem.

Mixed Folios

JOY TO THE WORLD & DECK THE HALL PLUS 15 TRADITIONAL CHRISTMAS FAVORITES
____ (F3138SMX) P/V/C
____ (F3138P2X) Easy Piano
____ (F3138P9X) Intermediate/ Advanced Piano (Roed)

17 of our most requested Christmas songs including: Away in a Manger • Bring a Torch, Jeannette Isabella • The First Noel • I Heard the Bells on Christmas Day • Joy to the World • O Holy Night • O Little Town of Bethlehem • Up on the Housetop • What Child Is This.

THE NEW HOME LIBRARY SERIES, VOLUME 6 — THE GREAT SONGS AND CAROLS OF CHRISTMAS
____ (THL1006C) P/V/C
____ (THL2006A) Simplified Piano
____ (THL3006A) All Organ

Over 70 Christmas songs. Includes carols, standards and popular songs such as: Have Yourself a Merry Little Christmas • Here Comes Santa Claus • I'll Be Home for Christmas • Let It Snow! Let It Snow! Let It Snow! • The Little Drummer Boy • Merry Christmas, Darling • Rockin' Around the Christmas Tree.

CHRISTMAS POPULAR & TRADITIONAL FAVORITES
____ (F3027SMX) P/V/C
____ (F3027P2X) Easy Piano (Schultz)
____ (F3027P3X) Big Note (Schultz)

A delightful array of favorite popular and traditional Christmas songs such as: Angels from the Realms of Glory • Birthday of a King • Gesu Bambino • A Holly Jolly Christmas • I'll Be Home for Christmas • Jingle Bells • The Night Before Christmas Song • Santa Claus Is Comin' to Town • We Wish You a Merry Christmas • When Santa Claus Gets Your Letter.

THE NEW CHRISTMAS FAKE BOOK
____ (F3021FBX) C Edition
____ (F3022FBX) Eb Edition
____ (F3023FBX) Bb Edition

A spiral-bound collection of 152 popular and traditional favorites. Includes: Angels from the Realms of Glory • Birthday of a King • Deck the Halls • Have Yourself a Merry Little Christmas • I'll Be Home for Christmas • It's the Most Wonderful Time of the Year • Joy to the World • We Wish You a Merry Christmas and more.

...and for Guitar

Aaron Stang/
THE CHRISTMAS GUITAR BOOK
____ (F3140GTX) Easy Solos with Tab

15 timeless Christmas songs carefully arranged to be easily playable by any guitarist. Includes tablature and accompaniment patterns so that the pieces can be played as duets. Titles include: Silent Night • Christmastime Is Here • The Little Drummer Boy • O Christmas Tree • Rudolph, The Red-Nosed Reindeer.

Jerry Snyder/BASIC CHRISTMAS SING BOOK
____ (F2487EGB)

47 traditional songs including: The First Noel • I Heard the Bells on Christmas Day • Jingle Bells • The Little Drummer Boy • The Night Before Christmas Song • O Christmas Tree • Silver Bells • Silent Night • Sleigh Ride • We Three Kings of Orient Are • We Wish You a Merry Christmas and more. Instruction included.